Breaking the Word
Reflections for Lectionary Readings, Cycle B

From the US, Megan McKenna is a well-known author, story-teller, theologian and lecturer. Previous publications include *Lent: Daily Readings*, *Lent: Sunday Readings*, *Playing Poker with Nana*, *We Live Inside a Story*, *Harm Not the Earth* and *The Hour of the Tiger* (all Veritas).

BREAKING
the Word

REFLECTIONS FOR LECTIONARY READINGS, CYCLE B

MEGAN MCKENNA

With gratitude to the monks of St Mary's Abbey, Delbarton, for their gracious hospitality, their shared prayer and community while this book was being written.

Published 2011 by
Veritas Publications
7–8 Lower Abbey Street
Dublin 1
Ireland
publications@veritas.ie
www.veritas.ie

ISBN 978-1-84730-327-1

10 9 8 7 6 5 4 3 2 1

'I Come with Joy' words by Brian Wren © 1971, 1995 Hope Publishing Company for the USA, Canada, Australia and New Zealand and Stainer & Bell Ltd for all other territories.

'Tree of Life', Marty Haugen, copyright © 1984, GIA Publications, Inc. Used by Permission of GIA Publications, Inc., Chicago, exclusive agent.

A catalogue record for this book is available from the British Library.

Cover designed by Dara O'Connor, Veritas
Printed in Ireland by Gemini International, Dublin

Veritas books are printed on paper made from the wood pulp of managed forests. For every tree felled, at least one tree is planted, thereby renewing natural resources.

Contents

The Season of Easter

Ordinary Time

Introduction

> As a magnifying glass concentrates the rays of the sun into a little burning knot of heat that can set fire to a dry leaf or a piece of paper, so the mysteries of Christ in the Gospel concentrate the rays of God's light and fire to a point that sets fire to the spirit of man.
>
> THOMAS MERTON

This book presents reflections, exegesis and quotes, together with questions for the Sunday and Feast day readings of Cycle B in the Lectionary. Cycle B is somewhat different to the other two cycles of readings, in that it is comprised of selections taken from both the Gospels of Mark and of John – split almost evenly between the two. These two Gospels are the first and the last of the four Gospels and so cover a range of perceptions of who Jesus is and what constitutes being a follower of the Way, bound intimately with the Word of God made flesh still dwelling among us.

For generations, the Gospel of Mark has been referred to as the Gospel of the Cross – the Wood of the Tree of Life that has saved us and has been transformed into a symbol of hope, freedom and resurrection. It was written during a time of great turmoil and persecution at the hands of Rome, when the followers of this new Way were defining themselves not primarily as being Jewish, but by becoming a new thing altogether. It was a time of fear and hope and new beginnings. The Gospel was written to prepare believers for Baptism, but with the vicious persecutions, it also served to call those who had betrayed their faith back to repentance and a sense of recommitment, to the waters of life and to the cross of discipleship. The person in the Gospel who most reflects this double intention is Peter, who is with Jesus as a follower and friend, yet betrays even knowing him and curses the name of Jesus. At the end of the Gospel, Jesus says 'go tell my disciples and Peter' (Mk 16:7): he too must learn to respond wholeheartedly to Jesus' words and to the challenge to take up the cross that is often the consequence of obedience to the Word of God in Jesus.

John's Gospel is universally referred to among theologians as the Gospel of the Word made flesh in Jesus, dwelling still among us in Word, Spirit and Body (which is both the faith community and the Eucharist). In a sense, Mark's Gospel is stark, immediate and straightforward in its demands and presentation of Jesus as prophet, preacher and Son of Man; while John's Gospel is layered, intricate and repetitive, doubling back continually upon itself to illuminate an idea or symbol. John's Gospel was written more than forty years after Mark's account and reflects a Church that is maturing, yet developing through the presence and the power of the Spirit in very different directions and understandings of the person of Jesus as the fulfilment of 'I am' statements that declare Jesus as God and as human.

Both Gospels are united in calling believers to renew their initial commitment to the following of Jesus' Way in the community of the Body of Christ here on earth in the power of the Spirit to the glory of the Father. Both are united in demanding integrity and constant faithfulness, and depth of understanding and enlightenment in what it means to be a 'new creation', the 'beloved servants and children of God' with Jesus, and to bring delight and glory to God the Father by the grace of the Spirit of Truth. And both are united in reminding believers of failure, of lack and of betrayal and how that impacts not only our individual relationships with God, but thwarts and divides the Body of Christ that is the community and dwelling place of God with us, in the Church and the world.

This book is meant to be a jumping-off place from which to hear, understand and perceive the Gospel as it touches each of our hearts and how it touches others within the Body of Christ today. Willa Cather, an American novelist of the last century, said about Church and the wonder of grace and power of the Spirit that is with us:

> The miracles of the Church seem to me to rest not so much upon faces or voices or healing power coming suddenly near to us from afar off, but upon our perceptions being made finer, so that for a moment our eyes can see and our ears can hear what is there about us always.[*]

---

[*] Willa Cather, *Death Comes for the Archbishop*, Book 1, chapter 4 (1927).

This book will be of use to those preparing sermons and homilies, those who are involved in the Rite of Christian Initiation of Adults, teachers and those preparing prayer services. It is hoped that it will also assist those in spiritual direction and in faith-sharing groups, so that those who meet to probe more deeply the Lectionary readings can draw forth their own responses to the proclamation of the Gospel texts.

If used in a group setting, each person can read the Gospel before they gather – a number of times silently to themselves and then aloud to hear the text in their own mouths and ears. When the group gathers, someone can read the Gospel and have a few moments of reflection. Sometimes it helps to take a minute or two to write down on a piece of paper (or in a journal) a word or a phrase that strikes one's mind or heart. Begin with that small piece: what does it stir within you? Why does it seem to touch you? What emotion or feeling does it call forth? Share these with one another. Then have another person read the text, this time listening for what you think Jesus is trying to express or what the text is actually saying. Again, take a moment or two to write or reflect and then share these with one another. As you share, try to identify what overlaps, or if the responses seem paradoxical, or if they follow upon each other. The depth and layering of the Gospel is inspired by the Spirit, and there is no limit to the Truth that is both revealed and concealed in the Word of God. The third time someone reads the text aloud, ask 'What in the text is disturbing to me or disconcerting, what doesn't sit easily or well with me?' This is referred to as 'the conversion question'. The Gospels are written to convert us, to move us from where we stand in mind, in heart, in will, and in practice, prayer, action and intent. They are given to us to transform us and to form us more into the image and likeness of Jesus crucified and risen among us. We are to become words of God in the world, echoes of God's Good News to others. And then, let everyone sit quietly for a few minutes and think seriously about what they will do this week to make this piece of the Good News of God become a reality in their life, work, study and relationships. Share this with one another.

This is the first half of studying and praying the Scripture. If there is time (the whole process doesn't take more than an hour and a half) read the text again – but think and listen as prophets! By Baptism and Confirmation and the power of the Spirit we are called to be prophetic witnesses to Jesus' presence in the world and to the words and practice of Jesus. Prophets are interested in what constitutes true worship of God, the care of the poor, and the coming of the realm of justice and peace for all on earth. These seem to us to be three different things, but for God and prophets they are three aspects of one reality. This time ask: what is the text exhorting us to proclaim as prophets to the Church and the world? Again, share the responses. Then – and this the question that is both the hardest to answer and yet the most revealing and conversional – ask, if this is the prophetic message of the Spirit among us, what we are going to do together this week to make this come true in our lives, our communities, our parish and our world? Lastly, ask the question: what in the text gives us courage and hope that God will do this work and make this come true in us?

This is the process. Sometimes the group will only get to the fourth question encouraging each individual to change something of import in their own lives; sometimes they will get as far as talking like prophets, but not moving into action; but the reflections should always end with the question about the Word and what gives us hope and courage to become God's words spoken and lived in the world today.

The initial quotes that begin each reflection can serve independently to provoke reflection or can be read in light of the exegesis and extension of ideas that follow. The questions are presented as both pastoral responses, prophetic suggestions and preaching arrows – pointers to your community, your parish, your relationships and your place in the Church and in the world. The Gospels are layered and limitless in the inspiration and power of the Spirit, and there are myriad ways of responding each week – especially when the Gospel is shared in a community, because the community that hears and struggles with becoming true to the Word of God is also inspired.

This book can also be used individually for prayerful reflection but its intent and hopefully its power lie in sharing it with others weekly, seeking to help one another to be true. We are the friends of God, the beloved of God, and we best reflect our God, the Trinity, in community: 'Friends are like pillars on your porch. Sometimes they hold you up, and sometimes they lean on you. Sometimes it's just enough to know they're standing by.' Together, we reflect God's presence stronger than anything we can do alone. May this book take you to the edge, and with your friends and the Spirit of God, help you to jump – to leap into the mystery of the unknown and the grace of God all around you, every day in your world.

To end this introduction, a prayer attributed to St Columba (521– 597) to draw us to stillness and instil in us the openness to approach the Word of God in our midst:

> O Lord, grant us that love which can never die,
> which will enkindle our lamps but not extinguish them,
> so that they may shine in us and bring light to others.
> Most dear Saviour, enkindle our lamps,
> that they may shine forever in your temple.
> May we receive unquenchable light from you
> so that our darkness will be illuminated and the darkness
> of the world will be made less. Amen.

Advent, Christmas and Epiphany

First Sunday of Advent

READINGS

IS 63:16-17,19; 64:2-7; PS 80; 1 COR 1:3-9; MK 13:33-37

> Gandalf: 'I am looking for someone to share in an adventure that I
> am arranging and it's very difficult to find anyone.'
>
> Bilbo: 'I should think so – in these parts! We are plain quiet folk and
> have no use for adventures. Nasty, disturbing, uncomfortable things!
> Make you late for dinner! I can't think what anyone sees in them.'
>
> J.R.R. TOLKIEN

We begin again, the year of the Lord 2012, and the great adventure
that is the mystery of the Incarnation – our God becoming flesh to be
born as one of us, to live and to struggle and die, and then to rise again
so that we might have life abundantly. For many of us, the beginning
of the Church year is about as welcome as it is to Bilbo's ordered life.
An adventure? No, thank you! And when we hear the readings from
Isaiah and from Mark we are often even more reluctant to plunge
headlong into the experience of God with us once again. In Isaiah,
we are immediately reminded that we have all wandered far from
God and our hearts have grown hard. And in Mark's Gospel we are
exhorted to stand up and face the Son of Man who comes with justice
to judge us all, with the warning that we do not know when the day
of reckoning will come upon us. This is not exactly what we want to
face in the deepening dark of late November.

And yet Isaiah cries out: 'Oh that you would rend the heavens
and come down, with the mountains quaking before you!' (Is 64:1).
And his hope is followed by another –that God will come and find us
doing right, ever mindful of his will for all in the world. The reading
flips back and forth: we are like withered leaves, forgetful of God,

reeking of guilt, and yet we are reminded that God is our father, a potter, moulding us into his very image!

And in the Gospel, we leap to almost the end of Mark's Good News, finding our beginnings in our end – standing with confidence, wide-awake, on guard and eager to welcome the Son of Man, the Son of Justice into our lives and our world. God is coming! God is already approaching near to us, bringing light, truth and peace as Holy Presence among us. There is an edge to the demand that we be on guard. Instinctively, we want to turn and run and yet we know that the best way to deal with what we fear is to stand and face it. Today it is time once again to stand our ground, lift our faces and look into the eyes of God in the person of Jesus, and to be seen truthfully for who we are and what we have become. Our God is coming, but we don't know exactly when. He is appearing in our flesh and blood, but we don't know exactly what that looks like. Anyone could be the one! Any face could look at us and we could see our own faces and souls reflected back to us. Your face, my face, that face could be the face of God.

Today we stop, reconnoiter, take a deep breath and step forward with our eyes wide open – looking for our God coming towards us. The adventure of God coming among us begins again. How will we meet God today, this week, this year? And will our God find us doing right and being attentive to the Truth, the Light and the Peace that is ready once again to embrace us?

Paul's letter to the Corinthians reminds us that we have each been richly endowed with every gift of speech and knowledge. Perhaps on this first day of the Church year, we should do a quick inventory: are we even conscious of the gifts that have been lavished on us? These gifts are given to us to share with others so that we abide in faithfulness as together we wait for ever-deepening revelation. Each year, with the Advent of our God among us, we are invited deeper into the mystery of the Incarnation, God in our flesh and blood, in our world and times as light and hope for us all. We approach these weeks as time to buy gifts, wrap them, and hope for what we want; yet we already have gifts to share with each other. We are told that we lack no spiritual gift! All that we need is already found in our communities, parishes, among the friends of God. Perhaps this Advent we need to look more closely at those around us, to uncover their gifts and call them forth to share them with others. Their gifts were given to help us all be formed into vessels that hold Good News, the truth that can be passed around with food, faithfulness, freedom and hope. We are not to simply encourage one another, but together as Church, we are to be the presence/the present that God gives to the world and all its peoples in the Word made flesh among us.

QUESTIONS

1. It's Advent. Are you ready for the adventure to begin?

2. Are there any people you'd like to go on this adventure with as travelling companions for the journey?

3. We are to stand before the Son of Man who will give us a glimpse of who we truly are, as God sees us. Are you ready for that revelation?

4. All the gifts are hidden among us: are there people in your church that you know have gifts? How can you bring them to light?

5. Isaiah describes us as withered leaves, wandering away from the ways of God and wallowing in guilt. What areas of your life, your relationships and your work or study need a good dose of hope?

Feast of the Immaculate Conception of Mary

READINGS

GN 3:9-15, 20; PS 98; EPH 1:3-6, 11-12; LK 1:26-38

> If everyone were holy and handsome, with 'alter Christus' shining in neon lighting from them, it would be easy to see Christ in everyone. If Mary had appeared in Bethlehem clothed, as St John says, with the sun, a crown of twelve stars on her head, and the moon under her feet, then people would have fought to make room for her. But that was not God's way for her, nor is it Christ's way for himself, now when he is disguised under every type of humanity that treads the earth.
>
> DOROTHY DAY

We hear today the reading that will be proclaimed on the fourth Sunday of Advent, just before we celebrate the birth of the Word in flesh that dwells among us – the mystery of the Incarnation. This reading draws us back to the moment in time when God slipped into the world of history, and nothing has been the same ever since. It is a feast celebrating God's work in Mary, but we are told in the teachings of the Church that so much of what you can say about Mary you must be able to say about each and all of us, especially in regards to what is written in the Gospel. The belief statements about Jesus are given to us, to draw us deeper into the mystery that is the Body of Christ and to remind us of the amazing love that God has for each of us, and the whole human race.

We know so little about Mary – Myriam. First and foremost she was a Jewish woman, a woman of faith who lived on the promises of the prophets and honoured the law and the covenant. She saw herself as one of the people bound to God, singled out and chosen to belong to God, as the Jewish people were to be a light to the nations and a city that drew others to his wisdom and ways. She would have known the psalms by heart, praying them daily since so many of them were connected to daily tasks and to seasonal celebrations and remembrances of what God had done for the people of Israel. She would have lived from Sabbath to Sabbath, hoping for and in expectation of the coming of the Messiah, the One who would set Israel free from the Romans and show them that the presence of the Just One was with them always.

She was young, probably betrothed at twelve to Joseph of the house of David – a house that was once the clan of kings, but now mired in poverty and living under the domination of Rome, along with all the other tribes. She was from Nazareth in Galilee – a place later described in another Gospel as a place where nothing good comes from (Jn 1:46) – a place of little importance. She is presented in Luke's Gospel as the model of the one who is called and chosen by God's Holy Spirit to give birth to the Word. In a sense, this telling of the Incarnation is Mary's Baptism, the coming of the Holy Spirit upon her. It is the beginning of a shift in her life of faith, into following her child as a disciple with others who hear the Word of God and seek to put it into practice.

Later in the Gospel, Jesus will be told that his mother and brothers and sisters are outside waiting for him. They do not come in and Jesus does not go out. Instead, he turns to those gathered around him, listening to him speak, and says: 'Who is my mother, my brothers and sisters – anyone who hears the Word of God and puts it into practice is mother, brother and sister to me.' Mary, though she is his mother physically, is also called to follow him as a disciple and give birth to the Word, the Truth of God in her own flesh and life. Mary's holiness lies in this: that she obeys the Word of God and puts it into practice, as all believers and followers are called to do. In the story she is confused, not understanding what is being asked of her, but she obeys the Word of God and her journey in the Spirit changes her life and all history forever. She accepts the vocation, the call to be a mother and to give birth to this child of the Most High God, even though, we are told that she is deeply troubled by this announcement of what her life is to become by the Grace of God.

Mary will be a mother and she is sister and daughter, disciple among disciples, friend and follower; and her story is also our story. In this season of the light, the truth and the peace of God entering our world and lives, we too are visited by angels and are offered annunciations. God's Word and Spirit seek to overshadow us and draw us ever deeper into the mystery of the Incarnation. We too are asked to let God's Word seize hold of our lives and, though we may not understand all that this might mean for us in the future, we are invited to respond with the words of obedience and trust: 'I am the maidservant of the Lord. Let it to be done to me as you say.'

QUESTIONS

1. The angel leaves her and will not return. This is the season of angels asking for our response to the goodness of God at work, dwelling in our world. God still waits on our reply and our acceptance. Put into your own words your response to God's graciousness to you.

2. How can I welcome the Word into my life this year? Can I read the Gospels with others, seeking to understand more truly that God still asks us in freedom to be a part of the great adventure of healing and extending his reign of justice and peace in the world?

3. Mary was a nobody, barely noticed among the poor and the displaced. How can I begin to look and to see who is invisible and ordinary around me? God, it seems, hides still in the poor and the places that others often disdain. What place in the world today cries out to be noticed and given dignity and hope?

Second Sunday of Advent

READINGS

IS 40:1-5, 9-11; PS 85; 2 PT 3:8-14; MK 1:1-8

> There is perhaps nothing we modern people need more than to
> be genuinely shaken up. Where life is firm we need to sense its
> firmness; and where it is unstable and uncertain and has no basis,
> no foundation, we need to know this too and endure it. We need to
> recognise that we have stood on this earth in false pathos, in false
> security, in spiritual insanity.
>
> ALFRED DELP

The readings in this cycle throw us immediately into the presence of
the prophet John the Baptiser – one who can certainly shake up our
world! And we are thrown off guard by being thrown around in time
too. Last Sunday we began at the end with the presence of the Son of
Man come in glory to judge the nations, but who is judging us all in
every moment. Now we fall back to the opening lines of Mark's Gospel
that are arresting in their own way: 'HERE begins the Gospel of Jesus
Christ, the Son of God.' It is a peculiar sentence, an announcement.
The word 'here' initiates the Gospel's interruption of God into the
world so long ago and, at the same time, interrupts us in our own time.
The Gospel begins now, here, in our lives and desert places, with the
call to repentance.

John's call to us is to 'make ready the way of the Lord, clear him
a straight path'. The coming of God in flesh in our world requires
preparation so that we can see, for God has been among us and we did
not notice his presence. We are always stumbling in the presence of
our God yet we are more concerned with our daily routines, troubles
and small worlds. As of old, we are summoned to go up on a high
mountain and cry out at the top of our voices: 'Here is your God!'
Our God comes with power. As God has shaken the world with the
Incarnation, we must shake our world with this Good News! Just the
presence of the prophet was enough to stir the people of Judea, now

these words must stir us to stop, reflect upon our own Baptisms and turn once again into the Spirit's air of expectation and hope.

John is intent on getting the people to look past him to another who is already among them, and to be alert to one that is more powerful than any prophet. John, who towers over any other person of his political and economic reality, is humble, declaring that he is less than a servant before the one who comes. He is not even worthy to stoop before him and untie his sandal straps. What does this say about us? We are called to look around and to see with eyes washed out with the Baptism of repentance. But what are we looking for?

Isaiah is clear. Our God comes gathering, shepherding and bringing together all the scattered, the lost and the young, careful of those who give birth and feeding all. These are the signs of the nearness of God among us. These are the works of Advent: feeding the hungry, gathering the lost and those straying to the edges, holding with tenderness those who have been hurt, carefully tending to the needs of those about to give birth, those who are sick and weak, those who are elderly. We are to draw all the disparate and different into community, celebrating diversity and making sure that everyone is welcome among us. The work of Advent is comforting and forgiving, encouraging people with an image of God that is nurturing and strong – like a shepherd intent on making sure all his sheep are well taken care of and safe together.

This is the work of shaking up our Church and parishes, our town and cities and our world. It is a shock, as drastic as all the valleys being filled in and mountains brought low, rugged land made fertile and wastelands turned into broad swathes of cultivated land. Even the earth senses the nearness of God's human foot upon it and responds with wholeness and goodness. If we are to see and sense God's ever-growing closeness to us, then it must be reflected in our dealings with the earth and with one another before we can sense any shift in our deeper relations with God.

QUESTIONS

1. How do you deal with having your daily routines and relationships shaken up and thrown off their usual course?

2. John was a sight to behold in skins, shouting and crying. Will you be on the lookout for someone who will come to you with wild Good News of God's nearness to you?

3. Peter tells his community that time with God is not as it is with us, that one day is as a thousand years and a thousand years is as a day! Will one of these days be the one when you shift your own priorities drastically and turn towards God's desire for a new heaven and new earth?

4. This newness and repentance is revealed in us, in our politics and economics, in all places where the justice of God resides, and where we all dwell at peace in God's sight. Our ability to see God begins in our practice of justice. What can we do together to make justice more of a reality in our small valley, plain, or hillside?

5. Already we are reminded that glory dwells in our land, in our midst. Can you see it?

Third Sunday of Advent

READINGS

IS 61:1-2, 10-11; LK 1:46-54; 1 THE 5:16-24; JN 1:6-8, 19-28

> Because of Her Singing They All Went Away Feeling Moved, Feeling
> Comforted, Feeling, Perhaps, The Slightest Tremors of Faith.
>
> ANN PATCHETT

This is traditionally Gaudete Sunday – the day of rejoicing and singing, for God is near. It is the Sunday of pink/rose-dawn coloured vestments and a tinge of exaltation. The darkness is receding and the sun is just behind the mountains or about to rise from the sea and our God is that close to appearing in our midst! We must sing. We must rejoice heartily in our Lord and let God be the joy of our souls. The echoing refrain is that of justice. God has clothed us in a mantle of justice. The earth brings it forth like plants and God makes justice and peace spring up before all the nations of the world. The coming of God sings of freedom and liberation, release of prisoners and a year of favour given to us by our God. The reading from Isaiah and from Paul moves, lifts us up and sings through us.

'And those who were seen dancing were thought to be insane by those who could not hear the music' (Angela Monet). In the Gospel we hear from some of those who cannot hear the music: some of the priests, Levites, leaders and teachers of the Jewish people who are sent to question John about who he is. And John is clear. He is not the one they are waiting for, he is not the Messiah, he is not Elijah or the prophet. He is the voice crying out in the wilderness seeking to make straight the way of the Lord. It is not what they wanted to hear. John's work is to help them hear the music, God's word calling them to change. To look for the light, to cease their ways that do not lead to the light, but cause people to stumble, even in the light. John dances to the Word of God even if it is not often heard, or understood or taken to heart. The sound of any word in a desert travels far and echoes over and over again. It comes at you from every corner, on the wind and bouncing off the sand. Are we listening and responding to that Word, urging us to dance, to rejoice in our God's demand for justice and peace?

John declares that he is here only to testify to the light. As children of God, that is why we are here too. And Paul tells his community just how to do that: rejoice always! Render constant thanks! Do not cease praying! Do not stifle the Spirit! Grasp the good! And it is God who will turn us inside out and make us truly witnesses to the light, promoting the presence of peace and unity in the expectation of Jesus, the Son of Justice, once again.

Our eyes are connected to our ears. An old rabbinic story tells us how we can know that the light has come. A group of disciples peered into the dawning light. One said: 'I know, you can tell the difference between a pear and a persimmon fruit.' Another said: 'I know, you can tell the difference between a friend and an enemy'. Still another cried out: 'I know, you can tell the difference between a wolf and a dog.' There was silence and the light slowly grew stronger, and their rabbi said: 'No, it is when you can look upon the face of every man, woman and child that you see and you can see the radiant light of God shining back at you.' John tells his questioners that there is one among them whom they do not recognise. 'This is the one that comes after me, and I am not worthy to untie his sandal straps' (Jn 1:27). We are in that same position today. There is one among us that we do not recognise. Both John and Jesus have been in their world for nearly three decades and so few see them for who they are. God is among us since the beginning and still so few of us see God in our midst.

Another ending to the rabbi's story goes this way: 'You will know that the light has come when in the face of every man, woman and child you can see reflected back at you your own face, the image and likeness of the Holy One; every glimpse of God, every sight of truth reveals our own life in its light and urges us to look upon one another with humility, with service and shared joy. God is so close. How do you know who stands beside you or approaches you on the street or is waiting for you to notice them?'

QUESTIONS

1. The familiar song of Advent 'O Come, O Come, Emmanuel' is not so much urging God to hasten, but reminding us that God is near, as close to us as our own flesh and every other human being's flesh and breath. Hum the song, hear the rhythm in your throat and heart and let it remind you to look to others and see that God is drawing near to all of us.

2. Paul's succinct prayer tells us that God will keep us, preserve us in holiness, whole and entire, spirit, soul and body, irreproachable, at the coming of the Lord Jesus Christ. This is the work that God is doing in us. How can you work with God to make us all holy?

3. How do you rejoice heartily in God and let God be seen and heard as the joy of your soul?

4. God has clothed us with a mantle of justice. Who in your environs needs to have that mantle thrown over them so that they can bless and praise God now?

Fourth Sunday of Advent

READINGS

2 SM 7:1-5, 8-11,16; PS 89; ROM 16:25-27; LK 1:26-38

> The angels of annunciation, speaking their message of blessing into
> the midst of anguish, scattering their seed of blessing that will one
> day spring up amid the night, call us to hope. These are not yet the
> loud angels of rejoicing and fulfilment that come out in the open, the
> angels of Advent. Quiet, inconspicuous, that come into rooms and
> before hearts as they did then. Quietly they bring God's questions and
> proclaim to us the wonders of God, for whom nothing is impossible.
>
> ALFRED DELP

Advent shifts this Sunday into immediacy – the moment of
annunciation by the angel Gabriel and the moment of the Incarnation
with Mary's acceptance, and the Word takes hold of her flesh! We
move backwards in time again, to the conception of the Light that
John the Baptiser is testifying to as the Gospel breaks into the world
of a young woman and nothing is the same forever after – for her, for
all the earth and for our history. And yet the rest of the reading from
Luke's Gospel is about the child to be born and who he is, who he will
be as a grown man, a human being in his history and place.

Theologically we are told these things: the child's name is Jesus
(which means 'the one who saves', like Joshua of old, who circled
Jericho until the city walls collapsed). He is great in dignity and will be
called the Son of the Most High. The sons of God were the prophets
and 'the' Son is the Prophet of God, interested in what constitutes true
worship of God, the care of the lost and the poor, and the coming of
the reign of justice and peace among all. The Lord God is his father and
he is of the house of Jacob. His rule will last forever, his will and way
will be honoured forever. He is the holy offspring of the Holy Spirit,
brought forth in the shadow of the Most High. The descriptions of
this child are staggering, hard to understand, in a word: unfathomable.
This is mystery unfolding into flesh and blood and bone, into a seed

in a womb, that will come forth as a child, born human and yet the Holy One of God.

We are told of Mary, the betrothed of Joseph of the house of David, the highly favoured daughter of God and blessed among women. And we are told that she is deeply troubled by the words of annunciation, not knowing what they mean. And still unknowing, yet hoping and believing that the impossible with God is the promise of life for all, she accepts whatever it will mean and declares herself to be the maidservant of the Lord. It is to be the same with us. The ancient stories are told to reveal God's revelation in the world then and, just as importantly, to declare what is happening and must happen among us now if God is to be conceived and born in our world. This is the impossible gift that is the way of God among us for all time. Now it is each of us that must believe in the golden seed of God, scattered by the Word of God to open our hearts and take root in our flesh. We are the announcing messengers to a weary world and we carry within our own souls and bodies the incarnation of God. This is the way the martyred Archbishop Oscar Romero spoke of it:

> Some want to keep a gospel so disembodied that it doesn't get involved at all in the world it must save. Christ is now in history. Christ is now in the womb of the people. Christ is now bringing about the new heavens and the new earth.

All this now depends on us. Mary can serve as a model but, as Church, all of us must make sure that the world sees us as embodying the Word of God in our flesh, carrying this hope of peace on earth with us as we make our way in the world. King David seeks to build a house for God to dwell in but God has another idea. God wishes to dwell with us, in our individual spirits and in our lives, shared and lived together. Just as Paul, in his Letter to the Romans, spoke of Jesus as Peace, Truth and Light, our communities and parishes are to be the dwelling place of peace, truth and light, a welcoming place for all the world. Now the angel waits for our response: 'Let it be done to us as you say.'

QUESTIONS

1. With whom are you building a house for our God? The time draws near – are the basics ready?

2. This mystery of the Incarnation must take place in our souls and bodies this year if God is to enter into our world. Are you ready to give birth to the Word of God in your life?

3. Angels are messengers and we are to be announcers of hope and light to the world. How are you going to do this in the coming week, alone and with others?

Season of Christmas

READINGS

IS 9:1-6; PS 96; TI 2:11-14; LK 2:1-14; IS 62:11-12; PS 97; TI 3:4-7; LK 2:15-20

The frightened shepherds became God's messengers. They organise, make haste, find others, and speak with them. Do we not all want to become shepherds and catch sight of the angel? I think so. Without the perspective of the poor, we see nothing, not even an angel. When we approach the poor, our values and goals change. The child appears in many other children. Mary also seeks sanctuary among us. Because the angels sing, the shepherds rise, leave their fears behind, and set out for Bethlehem, wherever it is situated these days.

DOROTHEE SÖELLE

Christmas has become universal, though different countries and even other religions emphasise and claim one detail or another for their celebrations. In Japan, for example, gift giving and decorations of snow and ice, glitter and glitz predominate, and one soon becomes aware that there is no child born, no glory of God sung round the world. And yet the wonder and the everlasting hope is still what captures the hearts of all who hear the story. As the carol, 'O Little Town of Bethlehem' says: 'The hopes and fears of all the years are met in thee tonight.' At midnight the story is told: a journey under duress, to be counted as animals belonging to another, one couple among many others, from a lineage once royal, now just poor; one child about to be born, not waiting for the time to be right or even easy. The birth is given in one line: she gave birth, wrapped him in swaddling clothes and laid him in a manger, because there was no room for them in the place where travellers lodged. We are familiar with the description and often get caught in the details, rather than reaching beyond to what the angels will proclaim to the shepherds in outlying fields.

The shepherds are the fringe folk, the outcasts – a group revered in literature and the spirituality of the Jews, with King David and even Moses coming from their ranks. But in reality they are shunned, humiliated and looked down upon. And yet, we often forget these are the ones that God decides will get the opening choruses of the Good News of the Incarnation, and these are the ones that God-with-us, Emmanuel is most at home with. We are told that this is what the kindness and the love of God our Saviour looks like, clothed in God's mercy. God lavishes attention and presence among those who are the least among us, still.

Christmas is the birth of the Word of God, Jesus, Word made flesh now dwelling among us forever. It is the emergence of God's revelation in flesh and blood, in history, in the limiting form of a child who will grow to be a human being, a man like any other, beset with human frailties, physical weakness, living out his life within a ninety-mile radius, dwelling his entire life with the eye of Roman domination ever-present, constrained by particularity – as all of us are in our lives. But the birth of this one human being declares that God is now walking with us, with each of us and with all of us in history and geography, bringing God's light, truth, justice and peace to be our companions along the way.

This is the birth of peace among us. The following is a prayer by John XXIII to pray this day and all days in this coming year of the peace of the Lord 2012:

> O Prince of Peace, risen Jesus, look kindly upon all humankind. It is from you alone that it looks for aid and rescue. Just as in the days of your earthly life, you always prefer the small, the humble, those who suffer. You step constantly in front of sinners. Grant that all may call upon you and find you that they may have in you their way, their truth, their life (Jn 14:6).

> This is our prayer, O Jesus: banish from men and women's hearts everything that could compromise their peace; confirm them in truth, justice, love for each other. Enlighten all leaders; may their efforts on behalf of peoples' well-being be united in the task with a view to ensuring them peace. Stir up the wills of all to overthrow

the barriers that divide us and to strengthen the bonds of charity. Stir up the wills of all to be ready to understand, to sympathise, to forgive; that all may be united in your name, and that in hearts, in families, in the whole world, peace, your peace, may triumph.

On this day, God gifts us with peace. Peace is given to all, it rests upon us as a child rests on its mother's breast and its father's lap; as friends and family sit at table to rejoice and strangers find they are welcomed in as friends. The sign of peace is a child wrapped in swaddling clothes, as he will one day be wrapped in burial clothes. This peace is found first among the poor and those who live on the edges of a society that says you must fit in, you must make it. We must learn the shepherds' way if we are to become those who are first to hear the angels, and first to see the child, and first to make their way back into the world with astonishing news – even for Mary and Joseph and all who would listen and take this Word of God, this sounding of peace into their hearts.

QUESTIONS

1. This child is called: Wonder-Counsellor, God-Hero, Father-Forever, Prince of Peace (Is 9:5). What is it like to look at this child and know a small bit of who he truly is? Pray to the child with these qualities.

2. This child will rule by judgement and justice, with zeal, breaking the chains of slavery, setting all who are bound free. This is God-with-us. What does this child want to do for you and yours?

3. We are now called 'frequented', not forsaken, the holy people – we belong to this Child of God. Can the child recognise us as his own?

4. Peace is God's gift to us, but peace is also our gift to each other. Are you giving peace out to everyone this Christmas, not in words but in deeds, in possibilities, in reconciliation and your presence?

Mary, the Mother of God

READINGS

SIR 3:2-6, 12-14; PS 128; COL 3:12-21; LK 2:22-40 OR 2:22, 39-40;
NUM 6:22-27; PS 67; GAL 4:4-7; LK 2:16-21

> It is through Christ that the power of divine love and the energy of
> divine light find their way into our lives and transform them from
> one degree of 'brightness' to another, by the action of the Holy Spirit.
> Here is the root and basis of the inner sanctity of the Christian. This
> light, this energy in our lives, is commonly called grace.
>
> THOMAS MERTON

Today is a surfeit of wonders and possibilities and yet it deals with
the light of one person, Mary as the Mother of God, and looks at the
naming of Jesus in the context of his family of Mary and Joseph. Often
this Sunday is referred to as the Feast of the Holy Family as a model for
all our families. And yet the readings, especially both Gospels, seem
to be trying to tell us that because of this Child Jesus – the Light, the
Truth and the Peace of God born to all of us – our families are not
just our blood kin, bound by marriage, children and affection. The
prophet Simeon, an old man who had the consolation and the power
of the Holy Spirit upon him, Anna, an elderly and faithful widow
constantly worshipping God, and the shepherds who visit Mary and
Joseph, seem to be a part of that family! This child binds together
those in faith, those who wait in expectation and live in hope and
those who long for and seek justice and peace for all. Because of the
Word becoming flesh among, us our families are not 'nuclear families'
consisting of mother, father and children, or even extended families
of cousins and related kin. No – now we are all the beloved children
of God, brothers and sisters to Jesus, all sharing the same blood and
word and bread connections.

Paul's letter to the Colossians tells us what our daily lives are to
consist of: bearing with one another, forgiving one another, acting with
mercy, kindness, meekness (non-violence) and patience. And it is love
that is to bind us together, as we dwell in peace with thanksgiving. We

are to be one in God, intent on keeping the family together. Today that means we are responsible for each other in the face of financial crises, political unrest and upheaval, change of jobs, status, familiar routines and amid the stresses of relationships that are experiencing unusual tension, lack and demands. Whether it's described as the 'Big Society' – the politics of balancing massive budget deficits caused by war, fearful responses to acts of terror, insecurity and fear – we are responsible for and with one another. Together we are to share our burdens and together we are to share our experiences of God's visits, presence and words of peace and hope. We cannot shrink into our small places where we are comfortable or feel we are somehow in control. Now our families expand and are diverse but are bound in the peace of this Child named Jesus who saves us all from our sins, insecurities and inadequacies.

The Gospel passage reminds us that amazingly, when the shepherds come to visit and see Jesus with Mary and Joseph, 'they understood what had been told to them concerning this child and that 'all who heard of it were astonished at the report given them by the shepherds'. Mary and Joseph learn from the shepherds and treasure the words and insights of these rough and realistic men and women who live in the open fields. These are the same shepherds who are often shamed and despised by their own people who are better off and consider themselves more religiously observant. Like Mary and Joseph, may we learn from those at the margins and come to recognise the wisdom of God in their midst.

Both readings end with the last description or image we are given of Mary, who in Luke's Gospel is the image of the catechumen, the young new believer before and after baptism. We are told that 'Mary treasured all these things and reflected on them in her heart' and that Jesus 'the child grew in size and strength, filled with wisdom, and the grace of God was upon him'. These readings are meant to be descriptions of each and all of us as well. We are to live, treasuring the Word of God no matter how and from whom it comes to us. And thus, with the child Jesus, we will grow in size and strength, be filled with wisdom, with the grace of God upon us. The Word of God has been seeded in us, and we are to continually give birth to that Word in our bodies and lives. We too, with Jesus, with Mary and Joseph are children of the Light, born of the Holy Spirit, and now our lives are to be a daily experience of being transformed from one degree of 'brightness' to another. Now we are reminded that we have found favour with God, along with Mary and the shepherds, and that we are now the bearers of peace, of light and truth to others in the world. Our lives are to be the cause of astonishment for others!

QUESTIONS

1. The reading from Numbers is an ancient blessing of God upon the people. Blessings are not just for priests, but we are all charged to bless others: parents, their children; husbands and wives, each other; friends, children of their elders in mutuality. Try this simple blessing on those in your own life: 'The Lord bless you and keep you; the Lord make his face to shine anyway and be gracious to you, the Lord turn his face toward you, and give you peace.'

2. It's easy to bless those we love. Who else in your neighbourhood needs a prayer or blessing? It can be verbal, but it can also come in a card, a shared cup of tea, coffee, or eggnog. Be creative and bless your world.

3. We are told bluntly: parents, don't nag your children; children, husbands and wives, obey! To obey is to listen and heed – it is a command for all. Our duty is to live in peace and to be peace for one another. How can you do that in your family and lives this year?

The Epiphany of the Lord

READINGS

IS 60:1-6; PS 72; EPH 3:2-3, 5-6; MT 2:1-12

> A vagrant, a destitute wanderer with dusty feet, finds his way down a
> new road. A homeless God, lost in the night, without papers, without
> identification, without even a number, a frail expendable exile lies
> down in desolation under the sweet stars of the world and entrusts
> himself to sleep.
>
> THOMAS MERTON

This is the day we have journeyed towards together. The season of
Advent and Christmas culminates in the Day of Light: Epiphany. The
word means manifestation or showing forth. This is the day the Light
bursts forth into the world, in spite of all that would block it or seek to
put it out forever. This day is troubling, disturbing, for it starkly declares
that not all people rejoice in the Light, or wish to be seen in the Light.
We are told in the Gospel that when King Herod hears that the One
who will rescue and liberate his peoples will be born in Bethlehem
of Judah, and that strangers come seeking to do him homage because
they have seen his star rising, he is greatly disturbed, and with him all
Jerusalem. When power is disturbed, all under its rule trembles too,
for the powers of the world do not wish to be displaced, even if the
threat is only a child born in the backwaters of an empire.

This day is one of jubilation and joy, of blinding glory and a light
that is far ranging and true, so that all nations can walk by its light.
Once again, we are told to raise our eyes and look about, to stand
radiant and let our hearts overflow and throb. And what we will see
will be people streaming towards this light, gathering, bearing gifts to
God. And this shining image is in sharp contrast to the shadows cast
by Herod and all power that dominates by destruction, war, torture,
random killing, injustice and poverty. The unsuspecting stargazers, in
their lack of knowledge about Herod, give him all he needs to begin
his search for the Star Child and to try to eliminate him as a possible
usurper and as a leader that will shepherd the people of God.

The terror of this story situates the soul journeys of the astrologers within the context of history, and those who rule the world through politics, economics and violence. The three original searchers leave Herod's court and the star appears again, guiding them to the place where the child is with his mother and father, safe for now. They do him homage and break open their gifts so that they can go home with empty hands and full hearts. But they have unknowingly set in motion a horror. Herod will use the information they eagerly gave him to wreck havoc on Bethlehem and slaughter any boy child under the age of two, unleashing grief and terror among all their families. This is the situation we all find ourselves in today as we seek out our relationship with God amidst the larger backdrop of history, politics, war, terror and torture, economic collapse and financial hardship. Like the three stargazers, we can easily play into the hands of those who are not interested for one moment in the search for God, or for hope for the downtrodden and poor who are today's victims of the world's lust for power and wealth.

In this season of dreams, angels and stars – all messengers of light and truth – we are drawn irrevocably to making decisions on where we stand in the world and who we stand with as followers of the Child of Light, the Son of Justice and Prince of Peace. The three foreigners are given a dream and go home by another route: having seen the glory and goodness of God they are also better at seeing evil and how it operates in the world: with cunning and lies, and with pretended interest. We must not be naïve either; we must know that we too should always seek another route through our lives once we have seen the Light of Christ and know the vulnerability of our God who comes as a child, an illegal alien, an immigrant. Anyone who is walking the edge of society's acceptability and falls through the deep and wide cracks in our countries and cultures are the faces of the children in the Gospel, innocents in jeopardy just because of their nearness to the Child of Peace. This child lives and escapes – for now. This begins the time between the cradle and the cross and it is our time too. The Light is loose in the world and the child will grow to be the shepherd of the people and the one who speaks the Truth. His very presence will be the Peace that provokes and the Light that reveals and lays bare.

QUESTIONS

1. Today all strangers and foreigners become a place where God's light can be seen, sometimes more clearly than among those who consider themselves to be believers and followers of the Light. Who is visiting you like the magi?

2. Epiphany is also a time of gathering and uniting, the beginning of a communion of believers that are diverse and yet bound in the Word and Light that is Jesus. Somehow we only look radiant with others, especially with those who are obviously different. Who in your life helps you to be radiant? And do you return the favour?

3. Stars give direction and a means of knowing where we are, but people are stars in that regard too. Who are the stars that help you steer home? Are you that star for others?

Ordinary Time (Sundays after Epiphany)

The Baptism of the Lord or the First Sunday after Epiphany

READINGS
IS 42:1-4, 6-7; PS 29; ACTS 10:34-38; MK 1:7-11

> Water facts: we are all water creatures. It makes up 60 per cent of our body, 70 per cent of our brain; and 80 per cent of our blood. We can go almost a month without food, but less than a week without water. The same amount of water that was available for drinking a billion years ago is the same amount available today, but now less than 1 per cent of fresh water is available for drinking – out of about 3 per cent that is mostly ice. Water connects us to the other elements: air, earth and fire, as well as to all other creatures and human beings. We forget often that water, along with all else God created and shared with us, is sacred and God expects us to take care of it and honour it.

We move immediately from the culmination of the bursting forth of the Light of God into the world at Epiphany to Jesus being made manifest and appearing in the world –being seen for who he truly is – at the moment of his Baptism. In the eastern Churches and in the early Church, three manifestations of light were celebrated: the Epiphany, the Baptism and the Wedding Feast at Cana, each showing forth the presence of Light, Truth and Peace in the world, the mature reality of the Word become flesh in the Incarnation, born of flesh on Christmas. And as the year of the Lord begins in what is called Ordinary Time – the time when we seek to absorb and begin to live out ever more fully, the mystery of the Incarnation in our own lives – we look at Jesus' Baptism and at our own Baptisms as the moment when we were drawn into the graced life of Light, Truth and Peace. It is also the time of being drawn into the communion of the Trinity – the Father, the Beloved Child and the Spirit.

The Gospel is short and intense. Jesus comes to be baptised by John in the Jordan; immediately, as he rises up from the waters, the sky is rent in two and the Spirit descends on him like the air under the wings of a dove. Mark's favourite word, 'immediately', signals that everything to come is going to happen quickly, strongly, unerringly. Jesus rises from the waters (resurrection) and the sky is rent in two above him. 'Rent' is another word of power – it only appears one other time in the Gospel, at the death of Jesus, when the veil of the temple is rent in two. But at this moment, all of reality is rent and torn apart. At this moment there is nothing that stands between us and God. The barrier has been forcibly removed. Now we stand with Jesus before God the Father.

And the Spirit descends upon him to remain with him. And now we hear again that voice, declaring in public: 'You are my beloved Son. On you my favour rests.' God is testifying to who Jesus is – beloved, son, child, servant (the words are almost interchangeable) – and that Jesus' very existence gives pleasure and delight to God!

In this moment all of creation is re-knit together in God. And we are given our first glimpse of the communion within God: the Trinity as it was in the beginning, long before the genesis of creation; and as God was revealed in Word, in Spirit, in God's continual expression in history, and especially in the life of the chosen people of God, Israel. But Mark's baptismal account echoes more specifically the words of Isaiah, telling us that Jesus holds the Spirit and is chosen for bringing justice to the nations, not letting anything vulnerable break or anything born of light to be extinguished. And he comes with strength, grasping us by the hand for the victory of justice, and we are formed to be light and to open the eyes of the blind and set everyone free. This is why Jesus is born and baptised and it is why we are born and baptised in the Trinity – to be light upon the earth in the eyes, hearts and history of all peoples

This account of Jesus' Baptism forms the depth of our own Baptism. Now we stand with Jesus, with the same relationship Jesus has with the Father, in the power of the Spirit and God says to us: 'You are my beloved, my child, my children, my servants. I take great delight in you!' We were created to give God delight! How are we doing? We begin our lives and now will walk the way with Jesus, pleasing to God, living in the Spirit, bringing hope and justice to all the nations.

QUESTIONS

1. Find your baptismal certificate and know the date, who your godparents are and where your life in the Trinity began. If you were baptised as a child, renew your promises of life with Jesus, to the glory of God, in the Spirit.

2. Our first baptismal promise is: do you promise to live forever in the freedom of the children of God? Like Jesus, we must live lives of setting others free, of bringing light to others and encouraging them and helping them to stay faithful. How can you do that today?

3. God in Jesus has 'grasped us by the hand for the victory of justice' (Is 42). This is why we were drawn into God's life. Share with others and ask them what they think being 'grasped by the hand for the victory of justice' means.

4. Water, as a verb, means 'to quench thirst'. What do you think Baptism makes you thirsty for, and that you need as often as you need water to survive?

Second Sunday in Ordinary Time

READINGS

1 SM 3:3-10, 19; PS 40; 1 COR 6:13-15, 17-20; JN 1:35-42

> Only connect ... Live in fragments no longer.
>
> E.M. FORSTER

Now, we move away from Mark's Gospel, the first one written, and into the Gospel of John, the last one written, with a gap of about forty years between them. Mark's Gospel is very short and so the Cycle B readings fill in many of the Sunday readings of the Lectionary with selections from John. We are still in the area near the Jordan, and Jesus is in Bethany. John the Baptiser is here once again, and when he sees Jesus he cries out 'Look! There is the Lamb of God!' Two of John's own followers are with him, and by pointing out Jesus to them he is shifting their attention away from him and towards the one he and all Israel has been waiting for. On hearing this, they both follow Jesus. We know from the next paragraph that one of them is Andrew, the brother of Simon Peter – but who is the other one?

This first encounter in John's Gospel of Jesus with others is layered with words that will often be repeated throughout the Gospel, and draws us into an initiation process shared with these two disciples and all those who seek to know and follow Jesus. They trail along behind him and it is Jesus who begins the encounter: 'What are you looking for?' But they don't answer, they come back with a question: 'Where do you live?' Here, the word 'live' has a deeper meaning – where do you dwell or abide? Jesus invites them into his world and life with the simple and direct words: 'Come and see.' We are told they stay with him for the rest of the day (from four in the afternoon – John's Gospel spans one day, from sunset at the beginning of the Sabbath to sunset the following day). So we know they spend their first Sabbath evening with Jesus, but nothing else is shared of that time together.

However, this evening sets in motion a series of connections. First Andrew goes looking for his brother Simon Peter and shares what he has found in Jesus – the Messiah, the Anointed, the Holy One of God, the long awaited hope of the people for justice, peace and liberation. This is exactly what Andrew was looking for, and by sharing his knowledge he brings his brother to Jesus. Jesus looks at him (the sense of being seen and known totally) and changes his name: 'You are Simon, son of John; your name shall now be Cephas.' There are at least six connections like this in as many lines.

Who are we when we are seen and known so utterly by Jesus? Cephas, translated as Peter, is often rendered as rock, but it is more like clay or mud that is malleable and can be changed again and again by water. When he acts as he did before he met Jesus, his name is Simon son of John; when he is acting as a disciple of the light he is called Peter; and when he is waffling and hesitant he is called Simon Peter. We have each been given baptismal names, as children of light, truth and peace. They are the names we are known by when we are followers of Jesus. John's Gospel asks us: What are you looking for? Who are you, really? What is your true name? Today is a day to let Jesus look at us and see us for who we truly are and look back in awe and wonder.

And the other disciple – who was he or she? Most people like to say that it was John, the beloved disciple, but it would be most unusual if it were and he does nothing in response to spending a Sabbath evening with Jesus. More likely, and more upsetting if it is the case, is that it was someone who was invited into the inner circle of Jesus' first disciples, but who did not connect and did not pass on that connection to others, and so continued to live a life of fragments and disconnections. The invitation is offered – how do we respond? To connect with Jesus must necessarily draw us forth to connect with others. Someone once said: 'A Christian is no Christian.' It is imperative for those who follow Jesus to follow him with others, to make those connections – first with family and friends and then with anyone who is seeking Jesus, as we are.

In the book of Samuel we hear the story of the Lord calling him, over and over again, while he sleeps and dreams. This is how our God is with us, always calling us. But we are confused, engaged in other things, unaware and so, often, we do not respond. Samuel is told to reply with these words: 'Speak, for your servant is listening.'

This echoes of our Baptism as the beloved servants of God; this is our beginning response in all times and situations, for God is speaking to us, calling us forth in every moment of life.

QUESTIONS

1. What are your baptismal names? What do those names mean? Are you becoming the inner root understanding of those names?

2. Andrew goes immediately to bring his brother Simon to Jesus. Who has brought you to stand before Jesus? And do you return that favour and bring others to stand before Jesus to be seen and known?

3. Samuel is instructed to respond to his voices, dreams and what disturbs him in his sleep, with the prayer of invitation to God: 'Speak, for your servant is listening.' Do we begin our days and end them with these words?

4. The verb 'listen' means 'to obey'. Once we listen to the Word of God, we are called to respond. The word 'listening' is applicable to the past, present and future – it becomes a way of life, a way of being present to God's Spirit and Word in the world. Don't listen if you don't want to change your life!

Third Sunday in Ordinary Time

READINGS

JN 3:1-5,10; PS 25; 1 COR 7:29-31; MK 1:14-20

> The Lord said: 'Follow me.' When you follow someone, you do not
> always see the face, but the back of the person. If you keep the Lord's
> back in view you will be following; the back can sometimes mean
> shadows and hardship – it is not always the light of his face. If you
> look in someone's face you are facing in the opposite direction.
>
> St Gregory of Nyssa

We are back at the beginning of Mark's Gospel and it begins ominously
with John's arrest and Jesus appearing in Galilee proclaiming God's
Good News: 'Now [today] is the time of fulfilment. The reign of God
is at hand! Reform your lives and believe in the good news!' God's
radical transformation of the world and history begins now in the
presence of Jesus among us. Jesus is acting in the ancient tradition of
the prophets, exhorting people to turn from their usual way of life to
another, totally different one. And he is calling people to come after
him, to follow in his footsteps along the way of justice, mercy and
truth. It is time to veer off the paths of evil, injustice, selfishness and
division and steer into his company.

The message of Jesus echoes the Word of the Lord that came to
Jonah in the first reading: to go and preach to a whole city, and to a
people that were sworn enemies of the Israelites. And yet, before the
first day is done, the city is turning, fasting and repenting of their evil
deeds and wayward lives. On this first day of Jesus' preaching he calls
forth two sets of brothers (we are most often called to follow with our
families, friends and co-workers). But first Jesus observes them, watches
them and assesses their interactions and way of life with others. Then
he summons them and they respond 'immediately'. Another word
that shocks us is that they 'abandoned' their father, their livelihoods
and work, their possessions and priorities – abandoned them! It is
as sudden and as sure as the people of Nineveh. A turnaround that
finds them in the same place, same relationships, same families, same

economic strata, same geographical location, and yet they are facing behind Jesus, becoming the companions along his way.

The readings are laced with immediacy and intensity. Paul tells his companions on the way that they are to live paradoxically – as they always do but with another intention and focus – in marriage, in the experiences of sorrow and joy, in business transactions. They are to live as though they are well aware that 'the time is short'. This too is part of the early Church's way of being in society. To do all the usual things everyone else does but to do them with one eye on the reign of God. And we know this consists of awareness of and care for the poor, the coming of justice, abiding in peace, being merciful and living together in union with the Word made flesh among us. These characteristics are what constitute the message of any of the prophets of old, as well as the prophet Jesus.

We are each and all called, chosen and invited into this Way, this power of God on earth now, this coming true of the Good News to the poor here in our corners of the world. But it begins with reforming our lives. A line from the Tao Te Ching reads: 'We shape clay into a pot but it is the emptiness inside that holds whatever we want.' Our being transformed into children of the Light, with Jesus, begins with emptying out our lives of what is superficial, extraneous and not in conformity with Jesus' Word. We begin this Sunday with the prayer of the psalmist and all the people of God: 'Your ways, O Lord, make known to me; teach me your paths ... you guide the humble to justice and teach the humble your way.'

In Mark's Gospel, each major move on Jesus' part will follow something violent or destructive that causes division and confusion and hurts the community. Today it is the arrest of John, who went before the face of the Lord to prepare his way. This is the shadow that falls along the way today. In following Jesus, we will know both the light of his face upon us, his company with us and the shadow of loss, fear, insecurity and danger as we walk with him. It is time to get used to the rear, the back of God going before us, leading us on.

QUESTIONS

1. Do you consider yourself a follower of Jesus? When did you first say 'Yes', though unaware perhaps of what you were getting into? Have you said 'Yes' again, lately? We must rise every morning and immediately set off again behind Jesus.

2. We are most often called within our families – with brothers, sisters, parents, even grandparents and cousins. With whom in your family do you share the desire to follow Jesus? We are told that James and John left their father in the boat with the hired help. Are there members of your family that don't share your need to follow with the same intensity?

3. In reality nothing external changes very much – they are still fishermen and they still go fishing, although now it will be with Jesus and they are to catch folk! If Jesus has caught you, whom have you caught for Jesus? Again, we rarely do anything alone – whom do you fish with?

Fourth Sunday in Ordinary Time

READINGS

DEUT 18:15-20; PS 95; 1 COR 7:32-35; MK 1:21-28

> Justice and power must be brought together, so that whatever is just
> may be powerful, and whatever is powerful may be just.
>
> BLAISE PASCAL

> Moses' vision of God began with light. Afterwards God spoke to him
> in a cloud. But when Moses rose higher and became more perfect,
> he saw God in darkness.
>
> GREGORY OF NYSSA

Jesus begins his public life in the synagogue of Capernaum, which
will become his home base. As a prophet, Jesus is interested in what
constitutes true worship of God and so he goes to the synagogue. But
he is also intent on caring for the poor and the outcast, the shunned
and the broken in body and spirit, and in bringing the power of God
to bear in all areas of life. First we are told that Jesus' way of teaching
has an innate power to it, a truthfulness and integrity that others do
not exhibit. This is because Jesus' words are embedded in his very
body, his being and person as the Truth of God made flesh. And the
people hear it and are drawn to it strongly, like a magnet – the core of
who each of us is drawn to the fullness of life.

Just two Sundays ago we heard in the words of Isaiah what Jesus'
work would entail: grasping people by the hand and claiming them
for the victory of justice. And that is precisely what he will do with
the man who cries out in the synagogue, shrieking and disturbing
the worship and the ability to hear the Word of God. He interrupts,
declaring for all to hear, whom he recognises Jesus to be: the Holy
One of God! Jesus sharply rebukes the man's spirit and with a simple
word of command: 'Be quiet! Come out of the man' (Mk 1:25). He is
released from the hold of what is destroying him and causing distress.
He is stilled. The man is described as having an unclean spirit (or in

other translations, as being possessed by a demon), meaning that he can no longer control his own behaviour, emotions and words. Something else overpowers his humanity and freedom. Whatever this possession or having an unclean spirit is, it is not, as is often portrayed in films, something that happens in an instant. It is the ensuing result of choices made – of choosing evil, choosing not to do good, of choosing not to get involved, of choosing to 'sell out', or of acting and blaming others by saying, 'I was only doing what I was told to do' or 'what everyone else was doing'.

Whoever this person is, he has abdicated his own authority or the power and authority of God and obeys powers that are destructive and disruptive. The people hear the power of true authority in Jesus' teaching, and even those who have become lost, manipulated and used by others and who sin can recognise who Jesus is: the Holy One of God. And Jesus' Word reaches into the man's soul, psyche and spirit and commands that he once again recognises himself for who he is: a child of God, belonging to God and called to serve and live in God's power of justice, of mercy and of truth. This is what Jesus is seeking to do with every word, every action and every moment of his life. Even evil can discern the presence of Good. At the time of Jesus, people believed that spirits were more powerful than human beings, but not as powerful as God. Today we refer to these spirits as addictions, dysfunction, habitual patterns of sin, destructive behaviours, or things we have done in the past that haunt us because we have not sought to right them.

In Deuteronomy, Moses tells the people that there will be another – a prophet that will reveal the Word of God, because they cannot bear to hear again the Voice of God. They are afraid that they will die.

Jesus, of course, is this prophet and more. This is the Word of God made flesh and dwelling among us. We do not die when we hear the Word of God in Jesus and encounter him, but something in us must die, must be transformed, let go of and radically altered. Jesus' very presence demands that we turn our attention and devotion to God first and foremost, reassessing all our priorities and ways of living, beginning with our worship. Like the people there, we can be amazed at this new teaching and authority, but like the man so divided within himself, we must obey the Word of God and make sure that we divest ourselves of all that does not serve God.

QUESTIONS

1. When you worship do you recognise the Holy One of God and listen intently to the Word of the Scriptures, the presence of God with you? Do you share that amazement and seek, with others, ways to put that teaching of Jesus each Sunday into practice?

2. Each of us is divided and distraught because of choices we have made and continue to make. We listen to God's authority in the Good News but we also listen to lots of other minor powers: the media, politicians, economists, fads in culture, our peers and contemporaries, the call to greed and selfishness, to rampant disregard for the earth and other human beings, to the misuse of other persons. Perhaps Jesus is rebuking us today. Are we listening? How will we respond?

3. Paul reminds his community that he only wants them and us to do all we can to promote what is good and whatever helps us to devote ourselves entirely to the Lord. This refers to an intensity of focus and the prioritisation of what is important in our lives. What and who helps you to become more completely devoted to the Good News of the Gospel? Try to be specific and practical and to endeavour to do that this week, not only alone, but also with others in your community.

Fifth Sunday in Ordinary Time

READINGS

JOB 7:1-4, 6-7; PS 147; 1 COR 9:16-9, 22-23; MK 1:29-39

> God wants a new poetry to be written, and is calling a new people to write it. And the name of the poem is 'The Kingdom of God'. This was what all Israel had been waiting for. It wasn't a new piece of advice. It wasn't a new political agenda. It wasn't a new type of spirituality ... It was the good (and extremely dangerous) news that the living God was on the move, and was indeed now coming into his kingdom. And it demanded a definite response. It was God's good news.
>
> Tom Wright

Mark's Jesus moves quickly after leaving the synagogue. The word 'immediately' appears five or six times in the first paragraph of today's Gospel. Immediately they leave the synagogue. Immediately they tell Jesus about Peter's mother-in-law being ill. Immediately he goes to her and grasps her by the hand. Immediately he raises her up and the fever leaves her, and immediately she begins to wait on them. Everything moves at break-neck speed. Jesus, the power of God, is loose in the world, reaching out and touching, altering everything and everyone in his path. The words convey power and a sense of being grasped, baptised, saved, called for the work of justice, being raised from the dead. And Peter's mother-in-law's response is that of service. The word used is that for a deacon who undertakes the work of the table and the care for the poor. In a few short sentences Jesus has his fifth disciple! The others were summoned from their work, but she (we do not know her name) responds and becomes a disciple out of gratitude. In fact, her house becomes the centre of Jesus' ministry, a house church.

Word spreads. Hope, the possibility of healing, the Word of God given freely to all with power, release from the burden of the past, of sin and guilt. Here now is a new thing, a poetry, a release of joy. And they gather at the front door, the whole town! This is Jesus' work and he responds wholeheartedly to the diverse needs of the crowd. And then he slips away to solitude, to being alone with God, in prayer. But soon they track him down – everyone is looking for him! And Jesus takes the God of his quiet, his listening and attentiveness with him and gets up to move on. His vocation, his life's meaning, is to share and give away God's graciousness in the Good News, especially to those who are in the most desperate need. So the short but powerful way through the towns, synagogues and roads begins. His disciples are to learn from his presence, his words, his gestures, actions, prayer, and even his absences.

Paul talks about what this is like: that preaching the Good News isn't an option or something to boast about, it's a compulsion, a drive born of the Spirit. He does it willingly but if he doesn't, he's ruined. He lives for one thing only: to share what he has been given – the Gospel of Jesus. And in the preaching he has been entrusted with, he finds that his freedom and power, even his imagination, grows so that he won't get in the way of the Word, but will serve it – knowing by the Spirit's inspiration how to approach very different people, giving them just exactly what they need by the grace of God. Like Peter's mother-in-law, he hopes to have a share in the blessings of God's kingdom.

What is this kingdom of God? The native peoples I have worked with have shared with me a way of speaking about it that might be evocative and new. It plays on the reign of God – of belonging to a power, an authority, to someone who you serve, obey and love in gratitude for all they do for you. It is also the rein of God that holds evil and sin and all that destroys people in check. It is a discipline, a practice that is strenuous and must be faithfully done with others. And it is the rain of God – male rain that comes hard and fast and furious (like Mark's outline of Jesus' work and life). It comes in spring and forces the seed into the ground. And female rain comes soft, hanging in the air in late summer, oftentimes not even touching the ground, but cooling the air. It is just enough to keep it growing in the heat, bringing it to maturity. Theologically, we are drawn into the reign of God at our Baptisms, into the Trinity and into the same relationship with Jesus that he has with the Father in the power of the Spirit. Such an amazing thing! It is the core of Jesus' teaching, and the heart of his power and life – it is meant to become the core of our hearts, our belief and practice and our life with God and others.

The reading from Job is dreary and bleak; perhaps it was chosen to describe what life might look like if there were no core, no heart to our lives and our belief. Just as we need air and water, we need to have a dream, a hope and a way that calls us constantly beyond ourselves and our day-to-day existence, or else we wither and die long before they lay us in the ground. We have been touched as Peter's mother-in-law was touched, healed, raised and grasped for the company of Jesus. We must ask ourselves if we have risen and have immediately begun to serve Jesus, his companions and the coming of the rein/rain/reign of God in our world.

QUESTIONS

1. When Jesus and his new followers leave the synagogue, they go immediately to someone in need of Jesus' Word, power, touch and presence. Where do we go after Church? Who is not present at our worship that needs what we have experienced and waits for us to come and visit them?

2. Jesus lives at the service of others, but rises early and slips away to pray. His time with God in the embrace of the Spirit is essential to his work, and is like the air he breathes, the water he drinks. Do we take the time to pray, to go aside and refuel and regroup, especially after we have been with a lot of people?

3. But at the same time, Jesus gets up immediately when he hears of others' need and goes out again, moving on to preach the Good News, to expel demons and to share the power of God with anyone who is in need. We don't have to leave home to do this, we just need to look around and begin to see who in our town, our place, needs to be waited on – like Peter's mother-in-law. It's that close to home and all around us.

Sixth Sunday in Ordinary Time

READINGS

LEV 13:1-2, 44-46; PS 32; 1 COR 10:31–11:1; MK 1:40-45

> Show me the suffering of the most miserable, so I will know my
> people's plight. Free me to pray for others, for you are present in
> every person. Help me to take responsibility for my own life, so
> that I can be free at last. Grant me the courage to serve others, for
> in service there is true life.
>
> CESAR CHAVEZ

Word spreads like wildfire through the towns and outlying areas so
that even those who are shunned by religious people, despised and
feared, blamed for their predicaments and illness, hear of Jesus' power
and that he does not discriminate. Even a leper hears of Jesus and
approaches him with a request. The very fact that this leper drew
near to Jesus, breaking one of the strongest taboos in society, reveals
his desperation. His request is an act of faith, leaving Jesus to make
the decision whether or not to heal him. 'If you will to do so, you can
cure me.' Jesus' reply is a mix of pity and compassion that breaks all
the laws of his religion and nation, and is born of his will: 'I do will
it.' This phrase reveals much about Jesus: his compassion, his reasons
for what he does, the power that he uses for God, his willingness even
to break laws and mores whenever they contribute to the pain and
isolation of others. It shows his single-hearted intent to be life-giving,
Good News to all, and to touch anyone – especially those others would
not touch out of fear or of lack of concern or neglect, using rules of
man-made religious practice or society's strictures as excuses. Jesus'
very nature and will is life for all, gratis and without any stipulations or
worthiness. He is the touch of God for those who are poor, who walk
the edges of survival, on the margins of acceptability. The leper breaks
the boundaries and approaches Jesus, and Jesus returns the favour
by breaking the boundaries and making himself one, in communion
with the leper.

This phrase reveals why and how quickly Jesus is judged with harshness because of the people he befriends, touches and draws into his circle. Jesus knows that if word gets out that he touched a leper, he himself will be shunned, excluded and he will be expected to do the rituals of cleansing before he can just be alongside others in 'clean' society. And he knows that the authorities in the religious community will react to his tender regard towards the leper, concerned that this itinerant prophet will usurp their power. So he tells the man to go and present himself for inspection and to offer in thanksgiving what Moses proscribed in the law. And he tells the leper not to say a word to anyone! But the man immediately goes off, telling anyone and everyone what Jesus has done for him, putting Jesus in the position where others now are wary of him, careful of him, and questioning his actions, motives and the core of who he is. And yet, now anyone and everyone keeps coming to him. Jesus is now a public figure, with all the problems and assumptions that go along with that notoriety.

That leprosy is a contagious disease, coupled with the widespread belief that one was punished with illness because of wrongdoing, made lepers both religiously unclean and righteously shunned, proclaimed by the religious authorities to deserve their sickness as punishment from God. They were not allowed into any area of society lest they contaminate others both physically and spiritually. And of course, there are 'lepers' still in today's society: those who are singled out to be shunned, condemned, blamed for their realities, as though they might be contaminated and make others impure, unclean and infected just by being in their presence.

And yet Jesus goes way beyond healing of the leper – he stretches out his hand (which wasn't strictly necessary), touches him and speaks with power and intimacy with him. This is the will of God and how we are to deal with those we have labelled 'lepers'.

QUESTIONS

1. This Gospel story can be very disturbing and unsettling because it confronts us with conflicts within our own society today. Who are the 'lepers' in the Church?

2. Paul tells his community that 'whatever we do' we should do everything for the glory of God and not give offence to others, no matter what their background. Specifically he says that we are not to seek our own advantage, but be attentive to others' needs. Which group of people do you find difficult to approach and to deal with compassionately, as Jesus did?

3. Jesus wills the leper's wholeness. At the time of Jesus, a person's will was thought to be found in their heart. So the very heart of Jesus wills the goodness, the holiness and wholeness of life for all others. How is your heart? Does it will the goodness and fullness of life, physically and as part of inclusion in a community? Do you pray for those who exist on the margins of society?

Seventh Sunday in Ordinary Time

READINGS

IS 43:18-19, 21-22, 24-25; PS 41; 2 COR 1:18-22; MK 2:1-12

> He is the hand of God's mercy stretched out to us.
>
> LEO THE GREAT

> A religion true to its nature must also be concerned about men and women's social condition ... Any religion that professes to be concerned about the souls of human beings and is not concerned with the slums that damn them, the economic conditions that strangle them, and the social conditions that cripple them is a dry-as-dust religion.
>
> MARTIN LUTHER KING, JR

Just getting through the first chapter of Mark can be exhausting! But now we spring into the second chapter on this last Sunday in Ordinary Time, before we turn to look to the season of Lent. And before we begin Lent, we are confronted with a story about an individual's relationship and connection to God, within the context of his friends, his community and the religious authorities of his society. Once again, the backdrop is set by the crowds of people pushing and shoving trying to get to Jesus. Jesus is back in the town of Capernaum, but it seems that this time some scribes have come early and they get the best, perhaps the only seats in the house. They were there to watch, to observe what is going on and what Jesus would do so that they could judge him according to their laws and traditions.

At this time, a house would commonly have been a three-sided one, a wall held upright by posts or a lower wall and covered with a roof of tiles, or just palm fronds for those who were less well-off. In this way, the house in Capernaum would have been open on the other sides, with people jammed in so that few could get anywhere near him. Jesus was preaching, and there were some very determined and creative people who would not let the crowd keep them from getting their paralysed friend into Jesus' immediate presence. So with some skill and ingenuity they climbed onto the roof, made a hole, removed some of the tiles and managed to lower their friend down so that he was right in front of Jesus. And it appears that this manoeuvre, so skilfully executed, thoroughly delighted Jesus. These were people after his own heart.

Jesus immediately responded to this evidence of both their faith in him and their concern and love for their paralytic friend. Aloud he declared to the man on the ground: 'My son, your sins are forgiven.' All hell broke loose, first in the minds of the scribes, and then in their hearts. They judged Jesus to be a blasphemer as no one was thought to have the authority to forgive sins except God alone. They said nothing, but Jesus saw them as he sees all of us – in the deepest recesses of their hearts – and he exposed them.

He set them a dilemma: which is easier – to say to the paralytic, 'Your sins are forgiven', or to say to him, 'Stand up, pick up your mat and walk again'? One wonders about their answer. What would you say? And what about us? What's easier: to be healed or to be forgiven? To heal someone or to forgive them? When I have asked this question of groups, practically all respond with 'Your sins are forgiven', though once, I was floored by a young girl who stood up and said: 'It's easier to tell the man to get up and walk again!' When I asked her why, she forthrightly questioned me: 'Do you know how hard it is to forgive someone, even for little things?' Really now,' she said 'sometimes I could just scream at how hard it is to forgive someone!' I was stunned – out of the mouth of this young girl came the truth rather than the easy, reactive answer.

But Jesus didn't wait for the answer. He told the man to rise and pick up his mat and walk again, to go home! And he did! The crowd was awestruck and praised God; they hadn't seen the likes of this ever before. I'm sure Jesus was hoping that the man's friends on the roof were staking their actions, their hopes and their love on the fact that if you can forgive someone, then you can heal them too if needs be. What's terrible about the story is that the scribes, and probably many others in the crowd, didn't want to deal with forgiveness – either their own need of it, or the responsibility of sharing it with others. This

Gospel is a good one to leave Ordinary Time with and step over the threshold into the season of Lent. Are we like the paralysed man, who has friends who will help him to be forgiven and to walk the way with Jesus once again? Are we like the friends who will go to great lengths to make sure those in need get to Jesus to hear his Word, and know his offer of forgiveness. Or are we like the scribes, caring little about the infirmities of others, deeming them deserving of such a condition because of how they have lived their lives? Or are we like many in the crowd who are amazed, and praise God, but are not moved to follow Jesus more closely after seeing what he does for others?

QUESTIONS

1. Isaiah the prophet declares: 'See, I am doing something new! Now it springs forth, do you not perceive it?' This new thing is the gift of forgiveness that heals us within and strengthens us bodily so that we can once again walk the way with Jesus that we were drawn into by Baptism. Do our lives reflect this new thing? Who needs to experience this in our attempts to help others?

2. Do you have a group of friends that you can rely on, who will draw you into the presence of Jesus, even at great cost to themselves in labour, time and risk-taking? Bless God for them and pray that you too are that kind of friend to others.

3. Paul tells his community that we are to say 'yes' always, no waffling about, no hesitation. We have made promises to God at Baptism, the second promise being that we resist evil and refuse to do harm. We can do that or break that promise, like the scribes, in our minds and hearts. We can do it through harsh judgement and the refusal to see and appreciate God's forgiveness and offer of strength to walk with him, no matter what others might think about us. This week, as we prepare for Ash Wednesday, what do we need to ask strength for and with whom will we walk on our journey?

The Season of Lent

First Sunday of Lent

READINGS
GEN 9:8-15; PS 25; 1 PT 3:18-22; MK 1:12-15

> We do not go into the desert to escape people but to learn how to
> find them; we do not leave them in order to have nothing more to do
> with them, but to find out how to do them the most good.
>
> THOMAS MERTON

> Any life, no matter how long and complex it may be, is made up of
> a single moment – the moment in which a person finds out, once
> and for all, who they are.
>
> JORGE LUIS BORGES

Today we begin together the great season of Lent. The word itself
comes from Anglo-Saxon, meaning 'springtime'; specifically it came
to mean the springtime of our souls. And the word also meant *lente* –
slow, go slowly, slow down, breathe more deeply, draw it out. We face
seven weeks before we reach the culmination of our lives as Christians
– the feast of the Resurrection, Easter. So the readings draw us into
the geography of the desert and, at the same time, draw us back to
water, to deprivation in the midst of what is alien to us (albeit with
its own beauty) and devastation by deluge. And yet both save! The
season is a time to relent, to stop and refrain from habits, from ways
of thinking, relating and behaving that we have grown accustomed
to or picked up unthinkingly from others, from our culture and from
what dominates our realities.

And we are introduced to the interruption of Satan – we are most
familiar with a medieval meaning of the word, 'the adversary', but a
better rendering of the word is 'hinderer' – Satan is anyone, anything,
any institution, structure, group, circumstance or system that hinders
us from being the beloved children of God, with Jesus in the power

of the Spirit, before our loving Father. Each of us can be the hinderer to others. Lent is a time for us to stop, stand still and become acutely aware of the ground we stand on, literally and figuratively, as Moses stood before the Holy One, and to take a moment to decide who we are, where we are and what it is we are to do in the world for and with others and in honour of the God who created us. We have a tendency to think of Lent as a time of singular turning through prayer, fasting and almsgiving, but we are called as a community to turn and to walk in the company of Jesus towards the week we call Holy Week – the offering of our living, dying and rising in the Body of Christ. Lent is time to remember these simple and profound words by Aung San Sui Kyi of Burma: 'We will get to our destination if we join hands.'

We go back to our beginnings in Genesis and hear again the story of the flood and the ark and all the living creatures that were saved to begin again – a re-creation story, a second-chance telling. God makes a covenant with us and with all living creatures, wild and tame, with the air, water, earth and fire within the core of our planet. Water will never again be used to destroy all mortal beings. It is a covenant of connections, of inter-relatedness of all things, of inter-dependence. It is right ordering of the universe and our place in it again and there is no word that we are to see ourselves as more important (except perhaps in our shouldering of responsibilities as we are images of God's creating and sustaining power) than all other things created. And the covenant includes us, the descendents of Noah's family. There was an ark made of pitch and bitumen. There is an ark today, made of the wood of the cross and the bones and flesh of the Body of Chris: the Word made flesh and all of us who are baptised, reborn into this Body.

We enter the desert with Jesus, not fearful, but as Jesus did – with the wild beasts, where angels wait on us. Yes, we will be put to the test by Satan, but it is a time to see who we are and to decide if we are truly the beloved children and servants of God as Jesus is. Will we accompany him on the way to the cross and to the glory of Resurrection? Will we decide if we will live out the Resurrection in our lives now? Are we to daily emerge with Jesus to proclaim with our lives that God's presence in Jesus has brought the power of God, its wholeness and goodness, to bear upon our lives and society? We are saved already, so now is the time to repent of anything that conflicts with resurrection life and to relent, here and now, to recommit ourselves to the covenant that God has made with us in Jesus and the Spirit.

QUESTIONS

1. The sign of God's covenant of enduring life was the bow in the clouds, the rainbow that can only be seen if you are standing in the right position to catch the refracting light. Are you going to stand in the Light of the Word of God in the Scriptures these forty days so that you can see more clearly what it means to reflect God's kingdom to others? Plan to make time daily.

2. Jesus dwelled in the desert with the wild beasts but there is no suggestion that he was afraid; he dwelled with them, as Adam and Eve did in the garden. How do we look at what is wild and untamable, at creation in deserts, the sea, all the geographical diversity of earth? All of creation reveals the goodness of God. Plan on taking walks, or find a park and be attentive to your piece of earth and sky, and, with Jesus, stand still and see God's revelation there.

3. Lent is for renewing covenants and practices that bring forth spring, for calling forth areas of our life to bloom again. What practice can you do for Lent that will share the Good News of the poor with others? With your deeds, proclaim that 'now is the time of fulfilment' for other people.

Second Sunday of Lent

READINGS

GEN 22:1-2, 9-13,15-18; PS 116; ROM 8:31-34; MK 9:2-10

> Look carefully around and recognise the luminosity of souls. Sit
> beside those who draw you to that.
>
> RUMI

> Sit with God as you might the ocean. You bring nothing to the ocean,
> yet it changes you.
>
> SEAN CAULFIELD

Traditionally the readings for the first and second Sundays of Lent
follow an ancient pattern: we begin in a desert and then go to a
mountain, the mountain of the Transfiguration, the place where
glory seeps through the veils of air and a glimpse of Jesus' true face
is seen shining. It may even be terrifying, yet it is a face of hope and
a signal of God's closeness to us. The word 'transfiguration' comes
from two words, the first a preposition in Latin 'trans', meaning across
or through, like a bridge, or a span over depths. The second word is
'figure', as in the human body. Together 'transfiguration' is a human
body that is a bridge across or through into another reality – Jesus'
human body, flesh and bone is the bridge through which we can see
and cross over into the presence of God in glory, Father and Spirit. It is
a moment that is fleeting but strong, as it imprints knowledge of Jesus
on the mind and soul. It is, like all brushes with mystery, a moment of
fear and attraction, a drawing in and a wanting to flee from the reality.
And, at its root, it is inexplicable.

The story is an echo of the coming of the Son of Man in the book
of Daniel, the image of a human being coming in great power and
purity to judge the nations with justice. He is human, and has suffered
greatly, and yet it is his suffering that gives him the power to judge
justly. It is an image of light, blinding, yet giving sight and seeing a
small iota of who Jesus truly is – the Son of Man. This is the image,

the name that Jesus uses to describe himself in all the Gospels – a mix of prophet, the Lamb of God, the crucified and Risen one, the Holy One of God and the judge of nations sent by the Father into the world for love. He appears with Moses and Elijah. Moses is the greatest of the Jewish prophets, the liberator of the people, leading them into the Promised Land (the kingdom of peace and justice) and Elijah is the prophet of fire, judgement and power. And both are turned towards Jesus in the centre.

The disciples are terrified – Peter almost babbles incoherently and is interrupted by the voice that is the Father, again speaking the words first uttered at Jesus' Baptism, now for the three disciples to hear: 'This is my Son, my servant, my beloved.' Revelation rendered. But now there is a command: 'Listen to him.' And there is only Jesus. The command for this week is to *listen to him* and to no other: not to the media; to those who tell us what we want to hear, who give us the easy way out; nor to those who cry for war, and selfishness, the politicians who are more intent on balancing numbers than caring for the flesh of human beings who reflect the glory of God for us. Listen. Sit still as though before an ocean, a mountain range, the night sky filled with stars, before the face of any human being.

Paul's word to his community is about this God who is for us, no matter who might be against us. This is our God who intercedes for us with the Father. This is the crucified One who lived with us, died with us, is raised for us and is with us forever as our friend and companion, our brother and servant. We have nothing to fear. Because of the Incarnation, the Body of Christ is as close as the flesh of every other human being – most especially the bodies of the poor, the folks on the fringe, the shunned and despised, those who experience what Jesus knew in his own life. All of these people are transfigurations, bridges in their own bodies that we can see through and cross over into the presence of the glory of God.

In Genesis we read of another covenant that God makes with all of us: a covenant of blessing, with countless people, and nations, for all those who will obey God's commands. The word 'listen' means 'to obey'. This week is for listening, for seeing and absorbing, almost by osmosis, the glory of God on mountain top and ocean's edge, but more closely, and in myriad forms, in the bodies of all the human beings who are God's gifts.

QUESTIONS

1. The disciples go down the mountains and they 'discuss' among themselves what Jesus' words might mean. We too must, on a weekly basis, discuss what Jesus' words might mean. But we must go beyond them: in the power of the Spirit we must make the Gospel a reality in our lives and make it come true in our decisions and deeds. If you aren't doing so already, start meeting with a group to study the Gospel for each Sunday and then seek to express it in your own life.

2. Abraham was put to the test. Ominous sounding, a 'test' reveals where we are strong and where we are lacking. He was asked for his only child and he was willing to give him back to God, who owns us all in truth. What do you think God would like from you this Lent? Is there anyone you cling to, wrap your life around, let influence you more than they should, or who has such a strong pull on you that in reality you relate to them as though they are God? Pray for anyone to whom you are so bound and share them with God, so that you can be friends of God together.

Third Sunday of Lent

READINGS

EX 20:1-7; PS 19; 1 COR 1:22-25; JN 2:13-25

> Christianity is being concerned about your fellow [people], not
> building a million-dollar church while people are starving right
> around the corner. Christ was a revolutionary person, out there
> where it was happening. That's what God is all about, and that's
> where I get my strength.
>
> FANNIE LOU HAMMER

For the following three Sundays of Lent we will shift into the Gospel of
John, which was written probably more than thirty or forty years after
Mark's Gospel and in the midst of the most vicious persecution yet
experienced by believers in Jesus. John's Gospel presents a Jesus who
is intent on dislodging the temple from its central place of worship,
casting doubt on the sacrifices performed there and calling the people
back to the only sacrifice that God wants of his people – the practice of
justice, mercy, forgiveness and truth, all born of love. Today's Gospel
is the only story that is included in all four Gospels, though in the
others, it is at the very end, seen as the last straw and the last piece of
evidence that the authorities need to condemn Jesus and hand him
over to the Roman leadership for death. But in John's Gospel it is placed
in the second chapter. From the beginning, Jesus is at odds with the
temple, its worship, sacrifices, power based in money and collusion
with Rome, and the injustices and insults to God that had developed
and flourished in its practices. It is near Passover – the central feast of
the Jewish people, celebrating their liberation from Egypt (the place of
bondage and slavery) and the start of their becoming the people of God.

Jesus is strong, powerful and uses force. Entering the temple
precincts, he attacks, as a prophet would, the money changers and
the sellers of the animals to be sacrificed in the temple. He does not
attack any person, only the tables – the economic system that would
make a profit from others' desire to offer sacrifice to God. We know
from exegetes that the money-changers would charge the poor more

for their lesser gifts of doves and pigeons than they would often charge for a small lamb, a more pleasing offering according to the priests. And so the system cheated the majority of the people twice, giving them a lesser offering when they had paid what others had for the 'more pleasing one'. There were, of course, many more poor people than people who had the money to spend on temple sacrifices. Jesus drove these hucksters out of the area, quoting the words of Jeremiah the prophet: 'Get them out of here! Stop turning my Father's house into a marketplace!' The more original translation better conveys the rage and dismay of Jesus: 'Stop turning my Father's house into a den of thieves!' And his disciples later (after the resurrection) declare that Jesus did this because he was consumed with zeal, passion and power for the honour of his Father.

Jesus is confronted by the leaders who want to know by whose authority he acts, but instead Jesus declares that his own body – the temple of God, the dwelling place of the Spirit – will be destroyed and after three days be raised up again. When John's Gospel was written, the temple had been levelled except for the western wall (the Wailing Wall) for more than twenty to twenty five years. So Jesus is not so much prophesying his death and resurrection here (though he certainly knows that this kind of behaviour will drive the authorities to want to eliminate him) as the Gospel writer is looking back in retrospect, long after the resurrection, and using the events that happened in Jesus' life fifty to sixty years previously to talk about contemporary experiences and to encourage his own community to act as Jesus did. They are to be faithful to the worship of God, as the Body of Christ, to the breaking of the Word and the Bread and to the sharing of that so that there are no poor among them and they are the presence of the Risen Body of Christ in the world now. The text ends with a more disturbing line aimed at his followers, declaring that 'he would not trust himself to them because he knew them all … and he was well aware of what was in every human being's heart.' We are left with that testimony: that we are known in the deepest recesses of our hearts. And we ask ourselves: does our own worship reflect the radical call of Jesus to right relationship and justice for all?

QUESTIONS

1. The first reading from Exodus presents us with the commandments of Moses that form the basis of life in community for the Jewish people. They are to worship God alone, and the way they deal with other human beings is as important as what they do in their worship practices. They are to refrain from anything that would once again enslave them to other idols and the false gods of society based on greed, violence and cult of their leaders. Look at the commandments and honestly assess where you are lacking in practice.

2. In the letter to the Corinthians we are reminded that the wisdom of God is Christ crucified, that this is somehow the power of God found in weakness. Jesus refused to accept the powers of the state: violence, war, slavery, greed, the denigration of the poor, a society built on fear, intimidation, torture, injustice and nationalism. For you, and those in your circle of family and friends, what does it mean to preach Christ crucified pragmatically?

3. Jesus is not interested in the outward trappings of worship – statues, gold vessels, marble altars, books, vestments and so on. Jesus is concerned with our hearts and will only entrust himself to someone who truly offers themselves to him and lives his passion and zeal daily. What is Jesus asking of you specifically this Lent? How can you join him in his zeal for the Father's honour?

Fourth Sunday of Lent

READINGS

2 CHRON 36:14-16, 19-23; PS 137; EPH 2:4-10; JN 3:14-21

> God has enough of all good things except one: of communication
> with humans God can never have enough.
>
> MECHTILD OF MAGDEBURG

> The followers of Christ have been called to peace. And they must
> not only have peace but also make it. To that end they renounce all
> violence and tumult ... His disciples keep the peace by choosing to
> endure suffering rather than inflict it upon others. They maintain
> fellowship where others would break it off. They renounce hatred
> and wrong. In so doing they overcome evil with good, and establish
> the peace of God in the midst of a world of war and hate.
>
> DIETRICH BONHOEFFER

Today's Gospel is a piece of the conversation that Jesus has under
the cover of darkness, when Nicodemus comes to visit and question
him. It has three vitally important lines and images that are shared
with us as we are deep into this time of Lent. The first is the image of
'the serpent lifted up in the desert so must the Son of Man be lifted
up, that all who believe in him may have eternal life'. Moses raised
the bronze serpent so the people could look upon it and see their
sin, and in repenting, be cured of their affliction. Jesus is lifted up on
the cross so that we can look on what we do to one another, see our
sin and insult to God, and be healed of our inhumanity and brutality
towards all made in the image and likeness of the Holy One. What isn't
in the reference is that eventually the bronze serpent was made into
an idol that the people worshipped, and it had to be destroyed. This
reference to the worship of idols is a theme throughout this cycle of
readings. Jesus went after the trappings of the temple worship because
they were worshipping the idols along with the outward rituals and
ignoring the Word of God.

The second line is: 'God so loved the world that he gave his only Son, that whoever believes in him may not die but may have eternal life.' This line is often separated from the one that follows it: 'God did not send the Son into the world to condemn the world, but that the world might be saved through him.' Sadly these lines and what follows are often used in the exact opposite way by Christians, to condemn and separate out who is saved and who isn't, to judge others harshly, forgetting that God is love. Christians have often taken these lines and used them as a battering ram to keep others out and consider ourselves 'saved' and 'in' with God. Sadly we sometimes use the cross and the Word of God as an idol, worshipping it out of context rather than changing our lives and being transformed by its power and suffering. We often use the objects that surround our rituals as idols, and get caught up in the object itself, rather than what it symbolises; for example, a gold chalice, rather than what it holds – the body and blood of Jesus.

The third line is the last of the reading: 'But the one who acts in truth comes into the light, to make clear that their deeds are done in God.' This is what we are to take from the Word this Sunday. Standing in the light of the Son of the Man, are our deeds worthy to bear the light? Christians are known by their deeds, by those they align themselves with and through their choices that publicly proclaim there is no other God but the Trinity, the community we dwell in. They live in gratitude and share the 'ever-more abundant life' that they have been given in Baptism (and Eucharist) with all, and especially seek to live as beacons of truth and hope among those who do not believe.

The reading from Ephesians begins with 'God is rich in mercy'. We have been saved by the kindness of Christ Jesus. God has given us his favour and recreated us so that we are his handiwork. We are to be intent on doing good deeds, not for what those deeds might gain us in return, but so that they can affect others and draw them to the life, love, salvation and kindness of God in Jesus. Because God so loved the world we must ask ourselves over and over: do we so love the world that we do not condemn and judge others, but share the mercy that we have been so lavishly given? We are approaching the cross, when the Son of Man will be lifted up. Will we be able to look upon the Son of Man and declare that we stand with him, no matter the cost?

QUESTIONS

1. The first reading from Chronicles covers the history of over a hundred years! Sadly it is a hundred years of unfaithfulness, of the worship of false idols, of despising the prophets and ignoring the Word of God. For those people the result is war, slaughter, torture, the loss of their children, the destruction of their place of worship, their dwelling places and leaders, and then their forced march into Babylon as slaves. The people did not honour their Sabbaths; they did not worship God – they lived like all the other nations. It is a litany of the ills of most of the nations of the world today, including those who claim to be Christian or Catholic. In what ways are our nations ignoring the prophets? Who are the prophets? Remember: a prophet cares, like God, for what constitutes true worship, the care of the poor, the coming of justice and that they are all of one piece. The only worship God wants is care of the poor and the practices of justice that provide peace and evermore-abundant life for all.

2. Nicodemus comes by night – he is afraid to let anyone see that he is even taking seriously what Jesus has to say, and yet Jesus shares the Light that he is in the world with him generously. Do we love the light that reveals the truth about ourselves, our families, our church and parishes, our countries? Or do we love the darkness more? Are we afraid to be associated with Jesus and so practice our religion only at certain times, or privately?

3. God so loved the world. Do we? Do people realise from our behaviours and priorities that we love, cherish, care for and nurture the earth and all that is created – the elements, all human beings, arts, culture, languages, religions? Reflect on how you, and those you live with, show forth that love of what is so diverse and varied, so wide-ranging and revelatory of God.

Fifth Sunday of Lent

READINGS

JER 31:31-34; PS 51; HEB 5:7-9; JN 12:20-33

> Tree of life and awesome mystery,/In your death we are reborn,/
> Though you die in all of history,/Still you rise with every morn./
> Still you rise with every morn./Seed that dies to rise in glory,/May
> we see ourselves in you./If we learn to live your story/We may die
> to rise anew./We may die to rise anew.
>
> 'TREE OF LIFE'

> Suffering is not overcome by leaving pain behind; suffering is
> overcome by bearing pain for others.
>
> DALAI LAMA

We are approaching the cross, and suffering and death, along with betrayal and torture, and Jesus is in Jerusalem when he says: 'My soul is troubled now' – a better translation is 'my soul shudders'. Jesus can sense the violence, the fear and lies that are swirling around the crowds and authorities in the city. He senses what is coming: his Passover. So many do not believe in him; so many reject him outright and seek to silence him. And yet there are outsiders, strangers, Greeks but believers, who come to Philip and say: 'We want to see Jesus.' And the chain begins: Philip goes to Andrew, and they both come to tell Jesus. We are all so intimately bound up with one another, especially in faith and in our search for Jesus. John's Gospel began with Jesus' words: 'Come and see.' Now there are some who have done just that, and Jesus knows that even though some have come to believe and to hear his Word, his time is growing short.

Each piece of John's Gospel is layered and interconnected. We can only look at one or two pieces, albeit superficially. There are Jesus' oft quoted words: 'unless the grain of wheat falls into the earth and dies, it remains just a grain of wheat. But if it dies, it produces much fruit'. He is speaking about his own life and death and what will issue forth – life beyond anything anyone could imagine. But he is also speaking about the 'us', the Body of Christ. We die together, all of us with Christ and in Christ and through Christ. This is the pattern of our lives, from the moment we die and are buried in the waters of baptism, the tomb of Christ, and all through our lives as we celebrate liturgy, until we rise again in the fullness of life with all in the universe.

Jesus is trying to both make his disciples face reality about the price of discipleship and to encourage them. What he says is amazing! 'Anyone who serves me, the Father will honour.' As the Father will honour Jesus in his life and death, so our Father will honour us, in our lives and in our deaths! Jesus is going to die horribly at the hands of other human beings, yet hidden in that horror is the glory of God. It is utter vulnerability, forgiveness, mercy, service and love unto death. Jesus shudders with the knowledge of what others will do to him and yet praises our Father and calls upon him to accept his life, his gift as the best he can give. Jesus loves his life in this world, and yet paradoxically in 'hating' it, he can give it away, lay it down so that even in suffering and death we will all know the depth of the intimacy and love that God is offering to us.

In the first reading we hear of the covenant that God made with the people after their betrayal and the disobedience that brought them to utter destruction, slavery and exile. With each covenant God draws nearer, moves in closer, and in this covenant it is no longer written on stone but in the hearts of all the people. Now anyone can know God, all people's sins are forgiven and God forgets the evil that has been done: 'I will be their God, and they shall be my people.' And now, in Jesus, we are loved by God our Father, in the power of the Spirit with Jesus, in Jesus and through Jesus. We are one body, one heart and one presence in the world; now we are called to glorify God with Jesus.

The letter to the Hebrews reads that Jesus reverenced God and that he learned obedience through suffering. Jesus wept, cried out, and prayed through his sufferings – he is the source of our hope, our being made human, made holy, made the children and servants of God. All of our life – its sufferings, losses, grieving, sadness – is drawn into the sufferings of the one we follow: 'Where I am, there will my servant be.' We are invited to be near to Jesus in his sufferings and death as well as in his joy and forgiving, his love and compassion. We are being invited to walk to the cross together, as the friends of God, and so to rise together too.

QUESTIONS

1. Some Greeks came to Philip. Some people come to us wanting to see Jesus. Do we know who to go to and then how to draw them to Jesus? That means facing the cross and the difficult things about following Jesus, as well as the companionship and knowledge of God the Father and the gifts of the Spirit.

2. More and more in John's Gospel, everything that Jesus says and all the images are in the plural. We must begin to see ourselves as part of a community, within communities, as the Body of Christ, wheat sheaves, as seeds sown together, as people living and struggling and dying and rising together. Do you have a community so that together you are servants of Jesus, with Jesus? Do you share the Word of the Lord together and serve others together?

3. Jesus will be lifted up, he will be tortured and crucified. The image of the early Church that was embraced was the cross, not a crucifix. We are saved under the sign of the cross – it is the wood and it is what we take up and bear, as Jesus did. We often get sidetracked in emotion and representations of the sufferings of Jesus when we are supposed to embrace the cross – the burden that is laid upon us because we live as Jesus did – for others, relieving their pain, stopping injustice and, when we can do nothing else, standing in solidarity and communion with those who suffer and die. Pick a group of people who are being crucified – lifted up in pain – this week and pray with and for them, helping them to carry their cross.

Palm Sunday of the Lord's Passion

READINGS

IS 50:4-7; PS 22; PHIL 2:6-11; MK 14:1-15, 47 OR 15:1-39

> The ultimate measure of a man is not where he stands in moments of convenience, but where he stands in moments of challenge, moments of great crisis and controversy. And this is where I choose to cast my lot today. There may be others who want to go another way, but when I took up the cross I recognised its meaning. It is not something that you merely put your hands on. It is not something that you wear. The cross is something that you bear and ultimately that you die on.
>
> MARTIN LUTHER KING JR

This is the week we call Holy. It begins in adulation, the waving of palm branches and a crowd that is jubilant, gathering for the feast of Passover – the feast of liberation and freedom. And it ends with darkness covering the earth, the shattering of dreams, the betrayal of friends and the death of Hope, the death of Jesus. In the intervening days lie all of life. There is suffering and joy, the extremes and the daily round of living. And all of it is holy, sacred and an offering unto God. The first reading pulls us back to the Baptism of Jesus, describing him as the one who speaks to the weary, rousing them, and as one who hears God's word and does not turn back. Instead he stands facing all those who would harm him and do him violence, setting his face like flint, trusting in God. It is an amazing and gut-wrenching act of abandonment to God that is paced out over days and nights, over a lifetime of faithfulness that is expressed in every bone and breath of Jesus. And it is to be so with us. And so we are told in the letter to the Philippians: 'Your attitude must be that of Christ'!

We are to look upon the suffering and crucified One who empties himself of his strength, endurance, breath and life. And in the midst of torture, pain and sorrow, even death, he is humble: that word means 'close to the earth', truthfully seeing oneself in perspective to all else and with everyone else, and with God. The bent and broken human being is Jesus Christ the Lord, the beloved of the Father, the dwelling and sanctuary of the Spirit. This is where the mystery of the Incarnation – God becoming flesh among us – leads, for as he has been born to us, and abided with us, so too he suffers with us and dies with us. God will exalt him and he will exalt us, but this is the week of losing it all, of being crushed to the ground, humiliated and left to die. This is the week to take a hard look at ourselves, as individuals, as Church, as those who call ourselves Christians or Catholics, and to see ourselves in this Passion account. How close to Jesus do we stand and align ourselves? How much distance do we put between ourselves and Jesus?

Martin Buber tells a story about human beings in agony and about God:

> Once a group of disciples came to Rabbi Pinhas to tell him of the terrible misery among so many needy and poor. First he listened, his head bowed, sunk in grief. Then he raised his head and looked at his disciples: 'Let us draw God into the world and all need will be quenched!' God's grace consists precisely in this, that he wants to let himself be won by humanity, that he places himself, so to speak, into human hands. God wants to come to his world, but he wants to come to it through men and women. This is the mystery of our existence, the superhuman chance of humankind.

This is the tradition of Judaism – the religion of Jesus. And we believe that in Jesus, God literally gave himself into our hands and that God still comes to us now in and through men and women. We believe that God wants to be drawn into the world and is in the world, found most clearly in those who are the victims of injustice and violence, in those who suffer at the hands of other human beings, and those who barely survive never knowing in this life what life ever more abundantly might mean for them. In Mark's account of Jesus' Passion is the story of Simon of Cyrene, pressed into service to carry the cross of Jesus. Every Holy Week all of us are pressed into service to carry the cross of Jesus. We walk the way with Jesus but we are called upon to look about us and see the sufferings of the Crucified One among us today. We are summoned to lift the cross from others, to bear one another's burdens, to ease the pain and suffering of others and to fill up what is lacking in the sufferings of Christ. Reflection on Jesus' suffering must lead to setting our faces like flint against the injustice, inhumanity and needless pain, and violent early deaths of so many. Otherwise we are just onlookers, waiting to see what happens, if Jesus comes down or if God rescues him. To be human is to be born, to live and to die, and Jesus shared all of that being human with us. Now we must live and die as he did, since we have been born with him and in him through our Baptisms. The Passion account ends with Jesus in the tomb. We begin this week seeking to make all of life, even death, holy, and living it with the Crucified One who is our Lord, our brother who calls us friends.

QUESTIONS

1. Take some time this week to read the Passion account by Mark slowly and reflectively. Make a list of all the characters besides Jesus: individuals and groups, even crowds. Where do you find yourself truly? And where would you like to be found?

2. We walk the way of the cross with Jesus and there is nothing we can do for him, but the mystery of the Incarnation is that whatever we want to do for Jesus, we can do for the Body of Christ and he takes it as done to him. Who is being tortured, suffering, crucified, humiliated in your country? Name them, pray for them and think and talk with others about what you can do for them, how you can stand in solidarity with them.

3. Jesus is crucified during the feast of Passover, the feast of liberation and freedom. This week is our Passover too, moving from all that hinders us from being and acting as the beloved children of God, who in all situations seek to rouse peoples' spirits and speak a word to the weary. In short, being hope in the world's hard times. What words of hope can you pray and share with others this week? Look closely at Mark's Passion account and at the words of Jesus. Reflect on one of them, and seek to put it into practice, imitating and keeping company with Jesus.

Holy Thursday, Mass of the Lord's Supper

READINGS

EX 12:1-8, 11-14; PS 116; 1 COR 11:23-26; JN 13:1-15

> A true Eucharist is never a passive, comforting moment alone with
> God, something that allows us to escape the cares and concerns of
> everyday life. Eucharist is where all these cares and concerns come to
> a focus, and where we are asked to measure them against the standard
> lived by Jesus when he proclaimed for all to hear that the bread that
> he would give would provide life for the entire world. But it will do
> so only if, finding ourselves with a basket of bread, we have peered
> deeply enough into the heart of Christ to know what to do with it.
>
> PAUL BERNIER

This evening begins the celebration of the Paschal Mystery, the heart
of our lives as Christians. It is a mix of deep abiding joy and equally
abiding sadness, with a sense of loss and gratitude. It is Jesus' Passover
meal that sets in motion his Passover from life to death, and his last
meal with his friends becomes the new Passover for all of us. So it
is the feast of freedom, and in Jesus' words, the feast of friends. In
John's Gospel there is no account of the breaking of the bread, and the
sharing of the cup; instead there is the shocking yet tender scene of
Jesus rising from the table, removing his outer garments and bending
before his disciples, kneeling to serve them, by washing their feet. This
ritual of washing another's feet was both commonplace and specific
in a country of dust, dirt, dung and feet protected only by sandals, or
often with no protection at all. It was an odious task, one that we don't
get much of a sense of when we do it ritually in church where people
have carefully washed their feet beforehand. But at the time of Jesus,
even a servant was not required to wash his master's feet, though on
occasion it was done by the host with guests, or by a husband and wife.

Jesus chooses the act of cleansing – the act of welcoming and
putting another at ease, the service of doing for someone what they
were used to doing for themselves as a chore, before sleeping, eating
or sitting down with guests. He does it to demonstrate how we are

to approach one another and live attentive to those around us. It is honesty, equality and care beyond what is expected, tender regard and an immediate intensity that expresses compassion and love in a public situation. It was a daily necessity, and yet could be practiced in such a way as to convey friendship, intimacy, respect and dignity. So it is crucial that we answer Jesus' question: 'Do you understand what I just did for you?' Jesus is teacher, Lord and the beloved servant and our God among us. And our God kneels to serve us and do the humblest and most servile task for each of us – this is to be our attitude and our practice towards all on earth. What our God does in bending before us, we are to do for others, and not just for those we love or care for.

One of the great preachers of the early Church, John Chrysostom, said: 'If you live alone whose feet do you wash, and do you dare to go to Eucharist?' And in another sermon he considers what feet washing might entail:

> To give alms is a work greater than miracles. To feed the
> hungry in the name of Christ is a work greater than raising
> the dead in Christ's name. When you work miracles, you
> are God's debtor; when you give alms, God is your debtor.

It is this reversal of roles and positions, this turning upside down of relationships that is the amazing and in some ways terrifying reality that we celebrate this day – 'as I have done, so you must do.' These words refer to what has just happened: Jesus washing our feet. But they also gather up all that he did in his life, as this, like bread, is to be given to others. The Eucharistic ritual is the taking, blessing, breaking and sharing of bread and wine, but the Eucharistic reality is taking it all, blessing God for all, and breaking up our lives so that all that we have been given is shared among those most in need, and then among our friends at the last, as Jesus has shown us.

We remember the Lord and his life, suffering, dying and rising by imitation. We often settle upon a ritual, or a moment in Jesus' life rather than endeavouring to gather up the entirety of our own lives (our resources, relationships, connections, possessions, everything) so that we can say this is our body, our blood, our guts, our dreams and it is all yours to use for others, O Lord.

And it is in this way that we remember the Lord. The gifts we bring – bread, wine, a collection for the poor – are to symbolise us, our bodies and blood and lives to be transfigured and offered as sacrifice (meaning made holy unto the Lord, for the Lord's use) and what happens to the bread and wine, happens to us – we become ever more truly the Body and Blood of the Lord to be shared in the world.

QUESTIONS

1. We often concentrate so intently on our individual relationship with Jesus that we forget, almost entirely, that Eucharist and all else in our lives as followers of Jesus happens in community. Jesus shared his last meal with his friends, the twelve disciples. It was a Passover meal, or one associated with the remembrance of the whole community, leaving bondage and setting out on the journey to freedom. And so it would be a meal shared and celebrated with families: the elders, women, children and friends. Who would you invite to your last meal?

2. Jesus wants to touch each of his friends' lives and so he washes their feet, and this is to be our way of life every day. Whose feet do you wash on a regular basis? Who do you serve and touch with tender regard?

3. How would you approach Sunday liturgy if instead of breaking bread and sharing the wine, we were each required to wash the feet of at least twelve others before we came to liturgy and to bring them with us? Share with your friends this week what Eucharist means when it takes the form of getting down on your knees to help others, rather than the usual ritual of Sunday mornings.

Good Friday – Celebration of the Lord's Passion

READINGS

IS 52:13–53:12; PS 31; HEB 4:14-16, 5:7-9; JN 18, 19

> One who has surrendered to it knows the way ends on the Cross –
> even when it is leading through the jubilation of Gennesaret or the
> triumphal entry into Jerusalem.
>
> DAG HAMMARSKJÖLD

> To choose the road to discipleship is to dispose oneself for a share
> in the cross ... It also means that we must regard as normal the path
> of persecution, and the possibility of martyrdom.
>
> US BISHOPS

It is Good Friday. It is the only day of the year when liturgy is not to
be celebrated, when we reflect upon the torture, crucifixion and death
of the Lord and look hard at our own participation and collusion
with evil that continues to wreak destruction on other human beings
in the world. It is a day of intense focus on those who walk the way
of the Cross with Jesus today, worldwide. It is when we take a hard
look at whether we find ourselves standing with the crucified and
seeking to uncrucify them, or whether we participate in adding to
the sufferings of others, adding our voices to the crowd that called for
Jesus' execution: 'Crucify him!' It is not an easy day for anyone who
calls themselves Christian.

It is the reading of the Passion according to John, and in it we
witness the confrontation: the stand-off between the powers of
domination in the world (Pilate) and the powers of the kingdom of
justice and peace (Jesus). Jesus' reply when asked who he is and why
he was born is blunt and utterly disarming: 'The reason I was born,
the reason why I came into the world, is to testify to the truth. Anyone
committed to the truth hears my voice.' And we must severely ask
ourselves whether we respond as Pilate did: TRUTH – what does
that mean? Are we too seeking to avoid any real encounter with the

truth that stands before us, condemning others to execution by the state, acting like a mob and even absenting ourselves from those we could help? And yet, still calling Jesus our friend? For Jesus' truth is clear: no violence or harm of anyone. In fact, we are to pray for our enemies and make them friends. It entails forgiveness extending to all, on every count, over and over again, as we have been forgiven. The truth is that all that we have been entrusted with is on loan and that we are expected, even commanded, to share it with those most in need, in gratitude to God. The truth is that there are to be no poor among us and that all are welcome in our company. We are all sinners and all in debt to our God for mercy that is continually extended to us. We all know something of the truth because we know Jesus the Word made flesh dwelling among us.

It is Good Friday because we are called to acknowledge the truth and to amend our lives and seek goodness for all in the world, especially those we have scandalised, treated inhumanly and kept outside the circle of the kingdom because of our sin. It is Good Friday because we are summoned to look upon the face and figure of the one who has 'no stately bearing, who is spurned and suffering, accustomed to infirmity, and from whom others hide their faces'. And we are thus summoned to look upon those in the world today who bear his infirmities. As Paul VI said: 'When will we come to realise that it is the poor that save us?' Similarly, John Paul II remarked: 'If you want peace, reach out to the poor.' Our God is found first and sadly in the so many millions of people still suffering today.

On this day, we do not celebrate Eucharist because our Beloved Lord dies. While in the past we did not share Eucharist, we commonly do so today – perhaps we need to be reminded that dying actually does remove that presence from our midst and, at least for one day, must fast not only from food but from the Bread of Life, in order to taste the death that was shared with us so that we could live forever. In any case, we need to make sure that our devotion and prayer is not just emotional reactions and empty words, but that we, as Church, make sure that others are not suffering and dying when we could help them, while we ritually grieve the death of the Lord.

QUESTIONS

1. The Gospel of John puts four people at the foot of the cross, witnesses to the death of the Lord. This is the community of the Beloved Disciples. Do we belong to such a community? When one cannot stop the violence and death of others, then we must stand with them in solidarity, put our own bodies in proximity to their bodies. This is where you find the community of the Beloved Disciples in the world today. Where are these communities? Do we support them, encourage them and on occasion align ourselves with them?

2. Joseph of Arimathea, a secret disciple out of fear, along with Nicodemus, comes and offers a tomb to bury Jesus in. They come late, but finally they come and acknowledge that they are connected to Jesus, in death if not in life. What do we offer to others in need – late perhaps, but finally giving what we have?

3. Jesus is buried in the tomb. There is the silence of death, of grief and emptiness. Take some time this day and tomorrow on Holy Saturday to sit with the depth of love that brought Jesus to be born among us, live and suffer and walk with us, and then, as his last gift, to die with us. Pray that with Jesus, in the grace of the Spirit, we will all hand over our lives and in our deaths belong to the Father. Then sit and wait, believing that even in death, our God is with us.

The Season of Easter

The Paschal Vigil, the Great Vigil of Easter

READINGS
GEN 1:1(2-25), 26-31A (31B-2:2); GEN 22:1-2 (3-8), 9A (9B), 10-13
(14), 15-18; EX 14:15—15:1; IS 54:5-14, 55:1-11; BAR 3:9-15, 32-
4:4; EZ 36:16-17A, 18-28; PS 104, 33, 16; EX 15; PS 30; IS 12; PS 19,
42 OR PS 51; ROM 6:3-11; MK 16:1-8

> 'Tis the spring of souls today; Christ has burst his prison; and from
> three days' sleep in death, as a sun has risen. All the winter of our
> sins, long and dark, is flying from his light, to whom we give laud
> and praise undying. Come to glad Jerusalem, who with true affection
> welcomes, in unwearied strains, Jesus' resurrection.
>
> JOHN DAMASCUS

> Easter is for all of us a dying to sin, to passion, to hatred and enmity,
> and all that brings about disorder, spiritual and material bitterness,
> and anguish. This death is indeed only the first step toward a higher
> goal – for our Easter is also a mystery of new life.
>
> JOHN XXIII

This night is one of fire and darkness and the shattering of it with a
single flame that is passed hand to hand. It is a night of storytelling
and the singing of psalms in response to the highlights of the telling.
It is a long night before we come to the proclamation of resurrection
and our new life. It is a night of water blessing and the Paschal candle
being plunged into the waters that will be used for Baptism. It is a night
of white garments given and promises renewed and then, lastly, it is
the night of the Paschal feast, giving thanks in the Eucharist, a meal
shared among tired and exalting friends. It is the heart of the life of
the Church, when we make new Christians; and as they are initiated
into the Body of Christ, we know ourselves to once again be alive in
the Risen Christ, by the power of the Spirit to the glory of the Father.

We stand together, new Christians shining with water and oil, with old Christians in joy, promising first to live forever in the freedom of the children of God. Second, we promise to resist evil and to refuse to be mastered by any form of death, evil, sin, injustice, violence or harm. And then lastly, we promise to live under no sign of power but the sign of the cross, the Trinity. It is a night of promises because our God has made promises to us from our very beginnings and has kept them all, in ways that we spend our whole lives seeking to understand and live out. It is a night that is singular for each believer and yet its power lies in the community. The Body of Christ – the Church – this night, more than all others, is known and experienced as the sacrament of the Risen Lord for all to see and be amazed at. Someone once said that the first hour is interesting, engaging with all the stories and elements of earth, air, fire, light, darkness, movement, singing and storytelling, but that the second hour becomes one of exhaustion, drifting, moments of insight, a bit of a marathon. And then the last hour or so is sheer exaltation, joy, singing, Eucharist shared, with eyes wide open looking at each other and seeing the Light of Christ shining on each others' faces. This is when all the Scriptures, all the moments of mystery that are the Incarnation begin to come together and we are overwhelmed and stunned into silence as we come to experience and know God made flesh, dwelling among us.

Mark's Gospel account is short, powerful and even disconcerting, because it leaves us hanging. The women go to the tomb to anoint the body of Jesus. In grief and trembling, they hear the gospel of resurrection – he is alive! They are deeply disturbed and run from the tomb in terror, and because of their great fear they say nothing to anyone! But Mark was wise. He was trying to impart to those who have never experienced the shock of the resurrection the disorientation and mix of unbelievable joy and fear that the reality of Jesus' being raised from the dead means for all lives. The women were commanded to go back to Galilee where they first met him and there they would see him. As they return with the disciples, Peter and all those who had come up to Jerusalem with them, they talk their way through their fears and share their experience of Jesus. And they come to know him in the Word and in their community.

The community of the Risen Lord is made by walking, talking and sharing the Word and Bread and life. This is the beginning of our Resurrection life – it begins in Baptism and the rest of our life is practice for its fullness in time and eternity.

QUESTIONS

1. The woman (three are named here, but at least eight are named in the Gospels) went to the tomb, worrying that it would be impossible to get in because of the stone. And yet, what they worried about was taken care of and they were the first to know that Jesus is alive! They sought to do a work of mercy, to prepare a body for burial, and they were blessed with the Word of God beyond their wildest imaginings. What works of mercy do you do, even in difficult situations? It seems that this way of living is part of the catalyst for the experience of the Risen Lord!

2. We hear the women told not to be afraid, for they come seeking Jesus of Nazareth, the crucified one. Who do we go with when we seek to do the corporal works of mercy, and where do we seek Jesus of Nazareth, the crucified one?

3. We are told that the women say nothing to anyone in their great fear, but how did any of us get here if they didn't say anything? Perhaps the answer lies in whom 'anyone' refers to: anyone who didn't believe in Jesus, anyone who would have turned them in to the authorities, anyone who hadn't gone with them to Jerusalem. They knew who to share this Word with: disciples, followers, friends, family and those who had been touched by Jesus. Who do you share this news with? Or do you keep quiet out of fear? We are the Body of Christ together. This kind of Good News must be shared!

Easter Sunday

READINGS

ACTS 10:34, 37-43; PS 118; COL 3:14 OR 1 COR 5:6-8; JN 20:1-9

> Let us dance with delight in the Lord and let our hearts be filled with
> rejoicing, for eternal salvation has appeared on the earth. Alleluia.
> LITURGY OF THE HOURS

> Faith in Christ's resurrection never misleads us, and hope in our own
> resurrection never deceives us, because God the Father both restored
> our Lord to life and will restore us to life too by virtue of his power.
> BEDE THE VENERABLE

This day of Easter is traditionally a day when many people return to
church, yearly or after a long hiatus, along with those who come every
Sunday. It is a gathering of the Body of Christ, made whole, made holy.
It draws many lost and wandering, half-hearted, searching and hungry
people back to the table, the Word and the community. We must be
mindful that this is a moment of grace spreading out into the Church
and all are welcome to the presence of the Risen Lord and to the
Church as the sacrament of the Risen Lord. Paul tells the Colossians
what each person who is baptised is reminded of as they come forth
from the waters: 'You have died! Your life is hidden now with Christ
in God. When Christ our life appears, then you shall appear with him
in glory.' Resurrection life – that mystery that we will look at for the
next seven to ten weeks, and then for the rest of our lives – begins in
Baptism, and the rest of our life is practice so that we live it more truly
each day and become the Body of Christ in the world more clearly
for others to see. If the letter to the Corinthians is used, then we are
reminded that we celebrate our Passover: our coming forth from the
tomb and the waters of Baptism into new life with bread made from
new yeast. We are now the unleavened bread of sincerity and truth.
We are the Body of Christ for others now to feast with and upon.

Acts' first great sermon tells us that we are witnesses to the Light,
to the person of Jesus, anointed with the Spirit, raised from the dead

by God the Father. We are told that he can be seen when those who believe in him gather to eat and drink with the Lord. He can be seen through the Word we preach, and the gift of forgiveness that we share with all. We are to be the people of joy! We are to greet and welcome all who come as the Risen Body of Christ this day.

The Gospel passage from John has the sense of confusion, of joy and terror, of those steeped in grief, disbelieving and not knowing what to think. Mary of Magdala and the women with her (she refers to those who were with her as 'we'), Simon Peter (his name when he is conflicted about his relation to Jesus) and the beloved disciple, never named in the Gospel. There is much running back and forth from the tomb, and then back home wondering, and back to the tomb, grieving still. Mary does not believe, Simon Peter does not believe; only the beloved unnamed disciple (hopefully meaning all of us) sees and believes. Mary is stuck in the past, wanting what was, who she thought Jesus was, and content to get her hands on the body of Jesus. Simon Peter is caught in the present, in the grip of his betrayal, his disowning and cursing of Jesus the night he was handed over to torture and death.

It is only the 'other disciple' who can see, and is open to the impossibilities of who Jesus might be. Jesus is not in the tomb, but as of yet they have not seen him and they have not yet begun to understand what might have happened, and how all of life, all the rules of existence, all of who God is in Jesus has been altered. This is Easter morning, the beginning of the mystery unfolding and the beginning of our resurrection lives together. We often stand in this predicament, 'as yet they did not understand the Scripture that Jesus had to rise from the dead'. During these next weeks, the Word will seek to enlighten us and together we will come to know more of what our Baptism means, and what it means to be in the presence of the Risen Lord, for the life of the world.

QUESTIONS

1. Resurrection is the culmination of the mystery of the Incarnation – God becoming flesh and dwelling among us. Now it is the Risen Lord of life who dwells with us. Take some time today to think about your Baptism and what it might mean. How does your life reflect the power of the resurrection now?

2. Are you like Mary, caught up in grief and sorrow, wanting what was, hanging onto your old, maybe even selfish and personal ideas of who Jesus might be and settling for a piece of that, even if it's dead? Or are you like Simon Peter, who can't see or understand because he carries too much baggage about what he did or didn't do? Do you need to let go of your failings and sin and believe in the forgiveness of Jesus' life and death and resurrection? Or are you striving to be like the 'other disciple', not named, who sees and begins a new life of light and truth?

3. Do you think of yourself as the beloved disciple running on ahead of others, even the leaders of the Church, but out of respect you wait for them to catch up? Love waits on authority and needs time to absorb the presence of God among us. Do you have others with whom you can share this awesome thing that God has done for us in Jesus? Other disciples who can strengthen your faith and help you to share, as you grow deeper in faith? Remember, this life begins at the moment of Baptism! Alleluia.

Second Sunday of Easter

READINGS

ACTS 4:32-35; PS 118; 1 JN 5:1-6; JN 20:19-31

> It is not possible to live and grow in the faith without the support
> of a group, of a Christian community. It is here that you will learn
> together to build a better world.
>
> POPE JOHN PAUL II

> Whatever we have comes from you ... Let us give with equally
> generous hands to those who are poor, breaking bread and sharing
> our bread with them. For you have told us that whatever we give to
> the poor we give to you.
>
> ALCUIN OF YORK

We begin the Easter season with the long version of this Gospel from
the Gospel of John and we will proclaim a shorter version at the end of
our fifty days of the celebration of the resurrection of the Lord, on the
feast of Pentecost. In a sense, this Gospel brackets the Easter season.
The appearance of the Crucified and Risen Lord takes place on the
night of the resurrection, when they are locked in a room, caught in
their fear. They have had any number of resurrection accounts from
the women of their company and disciples on the road, and yet they
are still paralysed in fear. They see him first with the marks in his hands
and side; he wants them to look at him and he greets them with the
first 'peace' of this story – the peace of the Father, and the peace that
remains no matter what happens in the world. And they go mad with
joy, hope and still some fear. And so he blesses them again with his
own peace, the peace of the Incarnation. Now he shares that, saying:
'As the Father has sent me so I send you', and he breathes his own
spirit, his life and truth, his power upon them. You can almost hear
the hush, the only response that can be made as God breathes on
them in Jesus' own breath, expelled in his last gasp on the cross and
now sent forth as power and peace. And this gift of his own breath
and life – the Holy Spirit – he gives to all of us.

And then the story is interrupted. They leave the room to look for Thomas, the one missing from their group, to share the Good News with him. And he is a wall, a block that stops the Good News cold. He won't believe them. He has his own criteria and it's awful: to see for himself and wantonly reopen Jesus' wounds, to make him bleed again. They only manage to get Thomas to come back with them a week later, and once again they are hiding in fear, in spite of all that Jesus gave them.

So Jesus comes again, and gives them the Peace of the Spirit that forgives and holds others bound for their lives and deeds. The peace goes forth to all of them, but he singles Thomas out for his stubborn refusal to believe the community. There is no mention of doubt: Thomas 'persists in unbelief' and in doing so he has stopped the power of the Spirit of God dead. Jesus demonstrates to the community how they are to direct the Spirit to speak the truth: hold others bound so that they can be broken from their selfish demands that stifle the Spirit and paralyse the entire community. There are far too many Thomases and Thomasinas in our communities, and in the days and weeks following the celebration of the resurrection of the Lord, we are to deal with them, so that the Spirit of God – given to us to forgive and hold the world bound – is set free. The Good News of God, the proclamation of the resurrection, is that we are all forgiven and bound again in communion with God. Jesus confronts Thomas, and using Thomas's own words seeks to make him admit his own disbelief and to recognise what his refusal to believe his community's announcements of the Good News has done to their faith. Jesus makes Thomas take responsibility for his words and actions. And we must stand in the Peace and the Truth and the Light of the Risen Lord, and deal with those among us who still block God's presence from setting others free. Jesus shows us that this is the strong Peace of the Spirit.

With the gift of these three powers of Peace – that of the Father, the Son and the Spirit – this day is also a day of rejoicing in the glimpse of the Trinity that we were initiated into at our Baptism, as we became the dwelling place of God; each of us the sanctuary of the Holy Ones and the place of the Spirit given to transform the world, as Jesus did. But we must remember it is all done in community. We must belong to a group of Christians that study the Word made flesh in the Scriptures, putting into practice what we have been taught, so that we become what we proclaim.

QUESTIONS

1. Acts gives us an incredibly simple and profound description of what these small groups of Christians are to look like still. They have, in this excerpt, only one startling characteristic, though it is repeated in three ways. All is to be held in common and shared with all so that there is no one in need among them. Being of one heart and mind comes from this sharing and giving. How do we share what we have so that others are not in need? What if the absence of this in our parishes and communities is the root of our divisions and the fact that we are not of one mind and heart?

2. The first sign of the resurrection is that there is no body in the tomb. All are seeking the body of Christ. The Easter season is the only time we do that in the liturgical year when we read the book of Acts straight through, because the Body of Christ is now among us. We are the Body of Christ and what we want to do for the Body of Christ we are to do for those in need: the hungry, thirsty, naked, sick, suffering. Together with your community or group, decide how to share with those in need around you.

Third Sunday of Easter

READINGS

ACTS 3:13-15, 17-19; PS 4; 1 JN 2:1-5; LK 24:35-48

> God is at home; it is we who have gone for a walk.
>
> MEISTER ECKHART

> Our Lord, who is truth itself, considers his WORD no less important than his 'Body.'
>
> JOHN MARY VIANNEY

Today we jump to the Gospel of Luke and read the last piece of the story of Jesus meeting with the two disciples who have left Jerusalem and are heading home to Emmaus. The very beginning of the chapter tells of the women at the tomb, who came to the other disciples with the wild story of resurrection and are met with disbelief. Then two disciples leave the city: one is named Cleopas, but who is the other one? Most exegetes now believe that it is his wife, Mary of Cleopas. She is also the blood sister of Mary, the mother of Jesus, one of the four at the foot of the cross in John and one of the women who went to the tomb in the morning to convince the apostles of what they had experienced. Jesus walks with them and takes them through the history of God's people and the prophets, and tells the story in light of his own words, deeds and presence. They are in despair, coping with the violence of religion and state that destroyed a man who brought possibility and hope to the people. Their hope was based on pieces of the story, but they left out the hard bits: the rejection, the despair, the horror of what human beings do to each other. They were running away from reality.

And Jesus begins to help them to understand, just as he has tried to do with all his disciples. We are no different. They cling to him and he goes in to have a meal with them. And they recognise him from his trademark ritual that he did so often on hills and mountainsides, where he fed multitudes without any regard for 'who belonged', just wishing to feed those who were hungry and wanted to eat. And the moment they recognise him, he vanishes and they run back to Jerusalem. They are met by many others and all excitedly tell their stories.

And it is here that the story is picked up: they recounted what had happened on the road to Emmaus and how they had come to know Jesus in the breaking of the bread. The next line is the core of the story: 'While they were still speaking about all this, he himself stood in their midst saying to them: Peace be with you.' Jesus is recognised in an instant and disappears in an instant at the breaking of the bread, but the telling of the story – the Word proclaimed – summons the presence of the Risen Lord that stays! How often have we ignored this part of the story, concentrating on the breaking of the bread and forgetting the breaking open of the Word, how it breaks open our hearts, bringing us back from despair to life, shattering the effects of violence and anything that has deterred us from believing in our God of life and truth and peace.

As in the Gospel of John, Jesus is intent on making them see him and his wounds, and so he eats with them. But he is even more intent on opening their minds to the Scriptures, as he did on the road with the two disciples. He will keep pulling them back to the word 'remember' (which was also part of his message to the women in the tomb). He opens their minds, draws them to understand: 'Remember those words that I spoke to you when I was with you; everything written about me in the law of Moses and the prophets and the psalms [that] had to be fulfilled?' And he makes them deal with the hard pieces of the prophets about suffering, dying and rising, about penance and the forgiveness of sin that is to be preached to all nations, beginning here and now today. This is what they are witnesses to.

These portions of Scripture are often referred to as the 'hierarchy of Scripture', the portions that take precedence over all the others: they include the Four Gospels, Acts, the prophets, the psalms and the first five books of the Bible. These take priority over all else and all the other texts are to be read in light of these, with the Gospels as the foundation.

Peter's sermon in Acts seeks to put into practice Jesus' words to go and preach this to all the nations, beginning in Jerusalem. We must today and for the rest of our lives as followers of Jesus give the same honour to the presence of the Risen Lord in the Word of God made flesh in the Scriptures as we do to the presence of the Lord in the Eucharist. It is in the Word shared that we summon the presence of Jesus crucified and Risen to dwell among us, so that his own Living Spirit can teach us, enlighten us and deepen our understanding of who Jesus is. When we gather to hear the Word in small groups and at liturgy our God is with us, always telling us: 'Remember all I told you.'

QUESTIONS

1. Peter tells his listeners that they acted out of ignorance and that now is the time to reform their lives and turn to God and be forgiven. We, as always, need to ask ourselves if we too are acting out of ignorance in any areas of our lives? It's time once again to turn to the Risen Lord, knowing we are forgiven, to seek to live our lives remembering and putting into practice what Jesus has told us. Do you belong yet to a group that reverences and studies the Scriptures weekly, with Jesus' Spirit teaching you how to understand its meaning and power in your lives today?

2. John writes in his letter to those who say that they 'know' Jesus and confronts them with the necessity of obeying and keeping the commandments that Jesus gave to us. If we know the Word, we must keep the Word and make the Word become the truth and reality of our lives. What piece of the Word heard today do you need to put into practice?

Fourth Sunday of Easter

READINGS
ACTS 4:8-12; PS 23; 1 JN 3:1-2; JN 10:11-18

> Live so that you bear outwardly as well as inwardly the image of
> Christ crucified, the model of all gentleness and mercy.
>
> PAUL OF THE CROSS

> May your luminous truth lead me and make me walk in your presence
> sincerely, with a perfect heart.
>
> GERTRUDE THE GREAT

This Sunday, we return to the Gospel of John and we will stay with
this Gospel until the end of the Easter season. Today is called Good
Shepherd Sunday because this is the image that Jesus uses to describe
his relation to us, the sheep. The first image reminds us of the Paschal
mystery we are still celebrating: 'I am the good shepherd; the good
shepherd lays down his life for the sheep.' This sentence uses 'lays',
the same word that we heard on Holy Thursday evening, when Jesus
rises from the table and lays aside his garments to go and wash his
disciples' feet. Jesus lays down his life in every moment of his living. It
is a handing over on behalf of others, the offering of his own person. It
is also the same verb that is used in Acts to describe those who wished
to be baptised when they laid all their possessions and lands at the feet
of the apostles and the community to be distributed to those in need.
As those baptised into the Body of Christ, our own lives are called
to reflect this 'laying down' in memory of Jesus, the Good Shepherd.

The second image reads: 'I am the good shepherd. I know my
sheep and my sheep know me in the same way that the Father knows
me and I know the Father; for these sheep, I will give my life.' This is
such an amazing statement! There is no limit to our being able to be
known by the Father or to know and understand the Father! God is
at home in us, as the Father was at home in Jesus and Jesus in God!
Later in the reading, Jesus reminds us that the Father loves him for

laying down his life for us and we are called to follow Jesus, laying down our lives for others. This language is all very theological, but what does it mean for us in everyday life?

In Acts, we read of Peter trying to explain to onlookers that a cripple that they see before them, now made whole and restored, was cured in the name of Jesus Christ, crucified and risen from the dead. Peter lives now by the power of Jesus' name. Always, he is preaching the One that he is still learning to follow himself, while being seen often as becoming another good shepherd in imitation of Jesus. Peter uses the image of the stone that is rejected becoming the cornerstone: the foundation upon which everything rests. In Jesus, the whole human race, and especially those rejected, exiled, excluded, condemned and pushed to the edges, are drawn back to the centre by the name of Jesus. Jesus, as the good shepherd, is intent on drawing all together in one flock, one community. He even reminds his initial followers (and all of us): 'I have other sheep that do not belong to this fold. I must lead them too, and they shall hear my voice. There shall be one flock then, one shepherd.' One of the primary works of the Church, as the Body of Christ, is to be this good shepherd in the world, drawing everyone together into community and unity and working to preserve that oneness in God.

Pierre Teilhard de Chardin said: 'Love is the only force that can make things one without destroying them.' This is the work of the Good Shepherd and our work. As John's letter reveals, we are the children of God, concerned about all the other children of God. We are the children of Light and the children of Truth. We are to feed regularly on the Word of the Lord, the strong presence of Jesus the Good Shepherd, still in our midst. We must be led back to the Word again and again, and together with others chew on the Word, absorbing it, becoming the words of God for others to take heart from and be drawn into with us.

QUESTIONS

1. The Shepherd knows us, but do we really know the Shepherd? Is it obvious to others who do not follow Jesus that we are the children of the Light and Truth, that we seek to heal, to make whole and to care for the cast-off, lost and straying sheep in a world with many hired hands and wolves? Are we listening weekly with others to the commands that Jesus had from his Father and obeying them?

2. We love the image of the good shepherd with the small, cute lamb in his arms, but in reality the shepherd was strong – able to withstand a wolf and carry a full-grown sheep on his shoulders. Shepherding is hard work; just keeping the wandering, easily spooked sheep together is difficult. Perhaps today we need to ask ourselves if we are still just wandering around going any which way, or if we are learning to be shepherds – or at least like the shepherd's obedient dog – working hard to keep the sheep together and safe?

3. Remember that sheep are not violent or aggressive and never use force to get what they need or want. They rely on the shepherd for food, water, good grazing, protection, companionship and leadership. Do we, with others, rely on the Good Shepherd, or do we more often than not selfishly go our own way, not caring much about the other sheep who are not of our fold?

Fifth Sunday of Easter

READINGS
ACTS 9:26-31; PS 22; 1 JN 3:18-24; JN 15:1-8

> John teaches how we live in Christ and Christ lives in us. Just as the
> trunk of the vine gives its natural properties to each of the branches,
> so, by bestowing the Holy Spirit, Christ gives Christians a certain
> kinship with himself.
>
> CYRIL OF ALEXANDRIA

> To be a follower of Jesus means in the first place to enter by
> compassion into his experience, with all that it expresses of the
> divine and the human. And it means in the second place to enter
> with him into the suffering and the hope of all human persons,
> making common cause with them as he does, and seeking out as
> he does the places of his predilection among the poor and despised
> and oppressed.
>
> MONIKA K. HELLWIG

This Sunday is about the vine, the branches and the fruit of the vine
that makes wine for the joy that others share together. The image is
the vineyard owner, the grower as the Father, Jesus as the stock – the
root of the vine and we as the branches. The unspoken image of the
Spirit is the Word that bears the life and power of Jesus through the
vine into every portion of the branches, and into the fruit. In these
Sundays of Easter, we listen to Jesus in the discourses of the night
before he died, seeking to tell his followers of the depth of his love, the
power that he is sharing with them and how intimately they and we
are drawn into his life and death and resurrection so that in the power
of the Spirit we all belong to the Father with Jesus. The vine and its
fruit are images found on many vestments, altar cloths and banners,
but we must remember what it's like to grow grapes, to trim severely
the vines and branches, paying painstaking attention to weather, water
and soil conditions. Even birds and other plants can destroy a crop
quickly. The longer they remain as grapes on the vine, the greater the

possibility of a good grape. And the older the vine itself, the better the grape and its produce. The vine is cut back yearly so it looks as though it's starting from scratch; in fact this makes it stronger and increases its yield. It is necessary for the vine to remain dormant for part of the year so that the grapes will be tastier. And of course, it's wise to remember that once it produces abundantly, it is crushed and made into wine for the delight of others.

In essence, this is what happened to Jesus in his own life, and so it follows that it should be happening to us as well. At the end of the reading we discover what a gift is given along with being bound in Christ. Jesus tells us: 'If you live in me, and my words stay part of you, you may ask what you will – it will be done for you. My Father has been glorified in your bearing much fruit and becoming my disciples.' We can stand before God with Jesus and ask for strength, grace and favour for others, mercy and forgiveness, communion and unity, and above all peace among us as we seek to image how God dwells in us and as the Trinity together. But we must let the words, the commands and hopes of Jesus stay with us, abide in us, dwell in us, as the branches abide in the rootstock of the vine.

John's letter to his friends reminds us pragmatically what that means: keeping the commandments Jesus shared with us and 'doing what is pleasing in his sight'. These words are echoes of Jesus' Baptism and our own, meaning that we exist and have been created to give delight to God, and that we do that best and most surely by loving one another. The reading from Acts brings us back to Paul's story of his conversion, as he tries to join the other disciples. They have long memories of what he did in violence and betrayal to the community. We hear of Barnabas, the disciple that wasn't chosen to replace Judas. His name means 'son of encouragement' and that is precisely what he is for Paul, and probably for many others. He leads and accompanies Paul, vouching for him among the others. Probably without Barnabas, Paul would never have been accepted within the larger community. It is certain that Barnabas would have been praying both for Paul as he stumbled into his new life as a believer, and for the community that was having trouble forgiving him for what he had done to them. Most of us aren't Paul (who certainly had his failings and weaknesses) but we can all be Barnabas – the sons and daughters of encouragement for one another, praying to our Father with Jesus in the power of the Spirit that the Church might be at peace, making steady progress in the fear of the Lord and enjoying the increased consolation of the Holy Spirit. Does this mirror our prayers in this season of abiding Peace?

QUESTIONS

1. The two characteristics of following Jesus, according to Monika Hellwig, are the two that Jesus was known for: compassion for and with others, and solidarity with those most in need or most excluded from the community. Who are the people, in groups or singularly, that you have the most difficulty being compassionate towards? And who are you definitely not in solidarity with but, like the early Church, tend to shun because of their past behaviours?

2. The Church was at peace: that simple statement carries a weight of wonder. The results are the Church being built up and making steady progress in the fear of the Lord and enjoying the consolation of the Spirit. Fear of the Lord, the last gift of the Spirit, is the gift of fearing to disappoint God more than you are afraid of anyone else – government, authority, even Church leaders or family. Perhaps we need to pray for this gift this week, and then we will know the consolation of the Spirit too!

3. John says: 'Little children, let us love in deed and in truth and not merely talk about it.' What can we do in small groups and as a parish community these weeks of light, joy and peace to make sure that our deeds reflect our belief in the Crucified and Risen Lord? In Psalm 22 we pray the lines: 'The lowly shall eat their fill.' How can we share some joy, some of the wine we have known through God, with others?

Sixth Sunday of Easter

READINGS

ACTS 10:25-26, 34-35, 44-48; PS 98; 1 JN 4:7-10; JN 15:9-17

To love another person is to see the face of God.

VICTOR HUGO

How can it be that even today there are still people dying of hunger? Condemned to illiteracy? Lacking the most basic medical care? Without a roof over their heads? Christians must learn to make their act of faith in Christ by discerning his voice in the cry for help that rises from this world of poverty.

JOHN PAUL II

This Sunday's readings are probably the heart of Jesus' teaching, and some of the most often quoted. Yet such familiarity can sometimes make them hard to hear, and harder still to understand. This is Jesus' sermon of the one commandment: love one another as I have loved you. It sounds upon immediately hearing it to be absolutely impossible. And yet Jesus goes on to say that there is no greater love than this: to lay down one's life for one's friends. We are all the friends of God and so, whatever we do for one another God takes it as done to him. This is the fullness of the mystery of the Incarnation: God abides in our flesh so intimately, that he would rather we showed our love for him in our care of other human beings, rather than in ritual or religious devotion. God, in turn, calls us friends! But it is clearly stated: You are my friends if you do what I command you. Do we do what Jesus has commanded us to do? The words of John Paul II make it very clear that as a whole, as Church, and as believers in Jesus, we're not doing very well.

We are to love as Jesus loves, and that means that every one of us – man, woman and child – will know in our actions, priorities and choices who we align ourselves with. They'll know through what we do with our resources, time, touch and even our prayers that we are the ones who move into the broken world to heal it, restore it, bring it peace and draw others together in communion. Jesus repeats the command again and again – the command I give you is this: that you love one another.

The reading from Acts reminds us that God's love is universal and is not based on our criteria or rules. God's Spirit moves and shows no partiality: any one of any nation who fears God and acts uprightly is acceptable to God. If only we remembered this and took it to heart. We need to begin to stretch our minds, our hearts and our lives to be amazed, and learn like Peter that God doesn't think or feel or act like we do, in limited or narrow confines or categories. The Spirit is loose all over the world, universally in all cultures, peoples, religions and places. It is we who need eyes washed out by the Spirit to see the working of God all around us. Like the early Church leaders, we must come to grips with the reality that the Spirit often comes before Baptism, not only during it or after it.

In our readings, we are beginning to hear more and more of the Spirit, since the time for the acknowledgement and celebration of the Spirit in our midst draws near. This Spirit is the Spirit of the Risen Lord, the Spirit of the Word made flesh dwelling in our midst in Word and Bread. It is the Spirit of Jesus the Christ. Jesus tells us to live in his love, and if we do, then of necessity we keep his words and command. Do we hold to the words, reverencing them, sharing them and listening to the Spirit in our small communities? Wherever there are words of encouragement, of forgiveness and reconciliation, of mercy and peace, of hope and truth, the Spirit is there. The Word of the Scriptures, like the Book of the Gospels lying open or stood upright on the table of the Lord, reminds us that our minds and hearts and lives must be laid open to all that the Spirit is trying to tell us. It is the Spirit that teaches us how to respond, how to act and how together to rejoice in the saving power of God in all nations and to all the ends of the earth.

QUESTIONS

1. The Spirit is everywhere in the world. Where do you hear and see the Spirit of God working? Try to make a list of people, of places and deeds that reveal this presence of God among us. Perhaps the Spirit trying to urge us to respond as these others do.

2. John tells his friends that love consists in this: not that we have loved God but that he has loved us and sent us his beloved as an offering for our sins. Jesus offered us life instead of death, forgiveness instead of vengeance, justice instead of injustice, peace instead of violence, mercy instead of self-righteousness and community with God and one another instead of selfishness and isolation. This is the only sacrifice God has ever wanted from us and it was given with Jesus. Now the Spirit of God chooses us to give that sacrifice today and to keep on giving it on behalf of others. During this week, look around you in the world and see where others are giving that sacrifice to God on our behalf and for all the world. Give thanks that the Spirit is working all around us.

Seventh Sunday of Easter

READINGS

ACTS 1:15-17, 21-26; PS 103; 1 JN 4:11-16; JN 17:11-19

> Those who bear the mark of the Spirit and the fire that Christ baptises with must take the risk of renouncing everything and seeking only God's reign and justice.
>
> ARCHBISHOP OSCAR ROMERO

> Prayers are threads and weaving in the breath of life.
>
> JOSÉ LEZAMA LIMA

This Sunday is a moment between Easter's joy and glory, culminating in the Ascension, and the moment of the Spirit bursting out into the world at Pentecost, shaking the foundations of life and all structures and peoples. It is about continuity in the midst of loss and failure but also about a radical break with what has been and what will be in the mystery and hidden knowledge of God. What connects these two momentous realities is prayer: the prayer of Jesus for us. In Acts, we hear how the Church gathered to replace Judas as one of the twelve. The Church is made up of about 120 people at this point. We are told of the eleven disciples, as many named women disciples, and, in Luke, of the seventy-two who are sent out in pairs and the families and friends that travelled with Jesus to Jerusalem. They take two who have been in their company from the beginning, Matthias and Joseph (known as Barsabbas, also as Justus and later renamed Barnabas). They draw lots (an interesting way to choose replacements!) and Matthias is chosen. Oddly enough, we know absolutely nothing about Matthias. However, it is Barnabas, the one not chosen for position in the structure of the Church, that becomes known as the companion and teacher of Paul, and a missionary preacher and friend to new members of the growing Church. This is one of the ways the Spirit worked in the early Church – choosing specific people, praying and casting lots.

The Gospel tells of Jesus' prayer before he leaves his friends to lay down his life and hand it over to God on our behalf. He prays for protection for all of us, and he prays that we might know his own joy and share it completely! Jesus says we do not belong to the world, we belong to God, and he prays that we remain in the world guarded by God. He asks his Father to consecrate us in truth. And as the Father sent Jesus into the world, now he asks that we are sent too. The first consecration is his own life and death and resurrection; ours begins in our Baptisms when we begin to live 'no longer for ourselves alone, but hidden with Christ in God'. It is a prayer that both reveals wisdom and wonder, and yet conceals more than we can imagine.

A note needs to be interjected here: when John's Gospel speaks about the 'world', it is not using the word as we do. It is not the world of creation and all that it entails in science, arts, culture, peoples, geography or other religions. Specifically, if refers to the dominating systems of injustice, violence or power that destroy life. These can be economic policies, racism, war, greed, rampant capitalism, any 'ism' that operates as an idol and any structure that confines, humiliates or takes away the dignity of human beings – such as nations, institutions and all organisational structures, including Churches.

How can we respond to this prayer of Jesus? Our lives are to be characterised by joy and by immersion in the Word. This means to be driven and sourced by the Word, to live with courage, knowing that no matter what happens to us, or around us, we are under the protection of God and our lives are to make holy all that we touch, experience and know in the world. We are to resist and stand firm against the world that twists and bends the Word of the Lord, and to live truthfully, with integrity as an alternative of hope. This is what it means to 'be consecrated in truth with Jesus.' This week, and perhaps every week for the rest of our lives, we could pray slowly again and again this prayer that Jesus prays for us throughout all of history on behalf of all the world.

QUESTIONS

1. Sit awhile and consider that Jesus is praying for you, for all of us, for the Church and the world all ways, always. What does that stir inside you? Share that with others and see how it strengthens your faith, and moves you beyond preoccupation with your own life, towards what God might dream and hope for all the world and its people.

2. We are told in John's letter that God dwells in us and that we remain in God through the grace and gift of the Spirit. This was one of the many gifts of our Baptism – to become the dwelling place of God, a refuge and a sanctuary for God, a temple of the Spirit, part of the Body of Christ, a beloved child of God and one of the beloved disciples of his own people. Pray and reflect on who you are and what God dreams for you in his Church and world.

3. The verbs 'abide', 'dwell', 'live in' and 'remain' are favourites of John. They are continually experienced awarenesses. Any verb ending in 'ing' reminds us of what has been, is and will be forever. They describe states of being that can deepen, grow shallow, shift and change but they cannot be eliminated. They have been, are and will be forever; they are states of being and can deepen, grow shallow, but never be eliminated. How can you describe this abiding, dwelling of God in you now?

Feast of the Ascension

READINGS

ACTS 1:1-11; PS 47; EPH 1:17-23; MK 16:15-20

> If you want to build a ship, don't herd people together to collect
> wood and don't assign them tasks and work, but rather teach them
> to long for the endless immensity of the seas.
>
> ANTOINE DE SAINT-EXUPERY

> Let us live by justice and by mercy and wait with bright hope for
> the Lord to come.
>
> MONASTIC LITURGY

This feast is a blip on the radar, a bump in the road, and it is often
celebrated on a Sunday (Seventh Sunday) because then it can be
properly observed, whereas on a weekday many cannot come. The
reading from Acts tells of Jesus' departure, telling his friends to stay
in the area of Jerusalem to 'Wait, for the fulfilment of my Father's
promise, of which you have heard me speak. John baptised with water,
but within a few days you will be baptised with the Holy Spirit.' We are
to wait, together, in trust, because God always keeps his promises, and
there is more to come. Jesus' work is not completed on earth until the
Spirit comes and is sealed in, to abide in all peoples and in all creation.

Ascension – to rise, to arise – is tricky to talk about and hard
to imagine. The reality of the resurrection, the ascension and the
coming of the Spirit at Pentecost is seen and experienced as one reality,
especially in the Gospel of John. Historically, resurrection, Ascension
and Pentecost happened in one day – the day of resurrection – but as
the Church grew the leaders adapted the Jewish calendar of Pentecost
and stretched it out into fifty days, breaking up the experiences and
the mysteries so that they could be absorbed more completely, and so
they came to be seen as separate moments. The friends of Jesus saw
him after the resurrection of his body, and though it bore the scars and
marks of his suffering and crucifixion, it was also a body resurrected
and full of light. They had to try to understand this new reality: that

he was alive and more alive than when he was with them in time and place. Then he tells them he is leaving! And continues to tell them that if he doesn't go, the gift of the Father cannot be sent and that this gift is far more true and more powerful than his risen body among them. They could not fathom it. How could anything be better than his risen presence with them? And that is the mystery and the challenge of this feast. No matter what happens with us in God; no matter what we know of God; no matter how much joy, insight, freedom and delight there is of God in our life, we must let go and not cling to it. We must always believe and trust that with God there is always more – more that is truth, light, peace, joy, knowledge, wisdom, power, grace and favour.

At the end of Luke's account we are told that two men dressed in white (like those who were in the tomb the morning of the resurrection) stand beside them and chide them: 'Why do you stand here looking up at the skies? This Jesus who has been taken from you will return, just as you saw him go up into the heavens.' Exactly what were they expecting? The words reveal two very demanding realities for us. First we are not to spend our lives looking up to the skies, concentrating on the after-life, or thinking that life here isn't crucial. No, we are to stand firmly on the earth, as Jesus did, and to make our way in the world, knowing that all is changed. One day Jesus will return, but this is not the point. The point is we are to stand and wait for the Spirit to come upon us so that we can live with the power and grace of Jesus here and now and until that day.

Unfortunately, the piece from the Gospel of Mark is an add-on to an add-on, and comes late in the tradition, long after the accounts in Acts or the Gospels. It is a mishmash of collected sayings. It borrows from Matthew many years later, and adds 'signs' that are hardly helpful to belief and the cause of consternation to many: expelling demons, handling serpents, drinking poison without harm and laying hands on the sick so they recover. The early Church may have had these signs in some places but they are not core to the power of the Spirit of God (with the exception of laying hands on the sick for comfort, strength and endurance in their suffering, recovery or death). And those who refuse to believe will not be condemned – as John has said, God sent

Jesus for love, for saving grace and mercy, not for condemnation. We should content ourselves with the words: 'Go into the whole world and proclaim the good news to all creation.' If we just do this then there will be signs, but ones that will have meaning for us today.

QUESTIONS

1. If we preach the Gospel, especially in deed and through the way we live in community for all to see, then there will be signs. Signs needed in our world today, such as peace, the absence of war, reconciliation, the cure for disease, hunger, drinkable water for all and respect for the earth. Where are these signs happening in the world? Who are the ones that are making the Good News a reality for the poor? It's time to think of ourselves as these signs, but for others' encouragement rather than our own.

2. What good experience or even understanding of God have you known or shared with others? Would it be hard to let go of that, so that God can grace you with something better, deeper and truer? Can you pray that you will stand before God with open hands for whatever blessings God might want to share with you?

3. Jesus is trying to tell his friends that the Spirit will come upon them and bring them something even better than his own bodily, risen presence. What could the Spirit bring to the Church today that is new, powerful and more expressive of what we find in the risen body of the Lord? Pray for imagination, creativity, possibility and wild hope for what the Church might need today.

Pentecost, the Day of Pentecost

READINGS

ACTS 2:1-11; PS 104; 1 COR 12:3-7, 12-13; JN 29:19-23

> I believe in the surprises of the Holy Spirit. The story of the Church is a long story, filled with the wonders of the Holy Spirit. Why should we think that God's imagination and love might be exhausted?
> CARDINAL LÉON-JOSEPH SUENENS

> The risen Christ, when he shows himself to his friends, takes on the countenance of all races and each can hear him in his own tongue.
> CARDINAL HENRI DE LUBAC

This feast is the culmination of the mystery of the incarnation and the resurrection and draws to a close the forty days of joy and exaltation when we seek to absorb what all this might mean for our daily lives as believers. As Church, we hear the story of the coming of the Spirit upon the Church, gathered in one place, and the symbols are all of power, motion, energy, transformation and interruption. There is noise like a strong driving wind; there is fire spreading out and forming into tongues of flame that come to rest on each of them. Their immediate response to the Spirit hovering over them is to express themselves in foreign tongues and make bold proclamations as the Spirit moves them. Try to imagine what this looked and sounded like! This is what is inwardly happening to us, as the whole Church is gathered this day. The Spirit is noisy and public, a shaking, driving and unsettling force, like fire hovering over our heads, as though our hair is on fire! It is one flame that separates, divides and yet in diversity is one, drawing others into communion and unity. The first expression is the ability to speak so that others can understand – the beginnings of dialogue, communication, listening and speaking in all the languages of those present. It seems God is not into uniformity but wild differences, especially and foremost in speech.

And they are driven to bold proclamations. The word 'bold' is one that is repeated often in the Book of Acts (the acts, deeds and experiences of the Spirit as it moves through the friends of Jesus out into the world). Each understands and hears the Word of God in their own language but does not understand the others. It seems the understanding of the Good News, the marvels of God among us, is essential for the hearers and that there is no way that sameness or one language can express the universality, vastness or depths of God's Word. What would the Church be like today if we prayed with bold proclamations so that all could understand in their own languages and dialects? There is more than one way to pray.

The letter to the Corinthians extends this vision to all the gifts of the Spirit to include vastly different ministries, works and manifestations. What binds them all is that they share in the common good and draw the Body of Christ together. The last line is a description of community: 'It was in one Spirit that all of us, whether Jew or Greek, slave or free, were baptised into one body. All of us have been given to drink of the one Spirit.' There were all those varying groups, but all were bound in the Word of the Lord. Whenever we want to drink deep of our Baptism and Confirmation again, all we have to do is return to the living water of the Scriptures.* All the images herein are of differences that make up one – a rainbow people, a rainbow creation.

And we hear again the first portion of the original ending of John's Gospel: the appearance of the cross-scarred Risen Lord, breaking through fear and locked doors to bring Peace to his friends, sending them out with the power of the Spirit – his own breath – to share that Peace with the world. The Spirit of God, the Peace of God, the presence of the Crucified and Risen Lord's own breath is given for forgiveness, reconciliation and mercy on the one hand, and to resist evil, violence, hate, injustice and despair on the other. This is the birth of the Church, it is the birth of the Body of Christ holding in flesh and Spirit all the peoples of the earth, and earth itself.

QUESTIONS

1. Today a Sequence, a prayer/psalm is often read or sung. It

---

* The tradition of all of Jewish theology is that the words 'living water' are code words for a long drink of the Scriptures, the Torah, the Word of God in the prophets. And so for us, the Gospels and Acts come first.

addresses God in so many ways: Holy Spirit, Father of the Poor, comforter the best, soul's most welcome guest, sweet refreshment, blessed light divine, grateful coolness in the heat, solace in the midst of woe, kindly Paraclete, giver of God's gifts. Take one of these descriptions and pray with it, letting the Spirit given this day teach you how to pray.

2. Along with the many ways of addressing God, the sequence also asks for many things the Spirit can do for us and to us: bring relief and consolation, bring ease, cooling grace, shine light into the darkest corners, wash clean a sinful world, rain down grace on parched souls, soften the hard heart, warm the ice-cold heart, give direction to the wayward. Which do you need today? What does the Church need? What does the world need?

3. Whoever the Spirit is, and however we seek to describe the Spirit, this presence of God is always about strength; energy; power; change; transformation; radical undoing and turning around; restoration and the cessation of all harm, violence, injustice, lies and despair. The Spirit is given for the big issues of the world, what to us often seem impossible. What impossible things should we be praying for today?

Ordinary Time

The Feast of Trinity Sunday

READINGS

DEUT 4:32-34, 39-40; PS 33; ROM 8:14-17; MT 28:16-20

> If we love one another and praise the Trinity, we will be faithful to the deepest vocation of the Church.
>
> POLYCARP OF SMYRNA

> To the Trinity be praise! God is music. God is life that nurtures every creature in its kind. Our God is the song of the angel throng and the splendor of secret ways hid from all mankind. But God our life is the life of all.
>
> ST HILDEGARD OF BINGEN

This feast of the Trinity is pure mystery. And yet in the Incarnation, we begin to know God as community, as communion and communication, as personal and intimate as well as vast, unknowable and beyond our ability to speak about with any surety. Whenever we try to describe mystery we resort to images, similes and words that break moulds and seek to open our imaginations and perceptions to newness and awe. Hildegard of Bingen, a mystic of the Middle Ages, calls God music, song and the splendor of secret ways. This introduces the idea of movement, sound, breath, notes, silences, pauses, even seemingly discordant sound or voices, a conductor, orchestra, solos – a variety of ways to try to speak of God. Whenever we speak of mystery, the first thing we become aware of is all that we don't know and that we are highlighting one aspect or one understanding. Mystery reveals and at the same time conceals, humbling us as we speak of God.

In the first centuries of the Church, the Greek word *perichoresis* was used in relation to the Trinity. It means 'to circle around'. It can be imaged as a Divine round dance, drawing in everyone and everything in a dynamic communion that never ceases. With this image, the

Trinity invites us, as it were, to 'come along in their company'. Icons of the Eastern Church have a number of images. The most startling one that I have ever seen was in southern Austria, though it was from another more Eastern Orthodox country and tradition. It showed Jesus sitting in the middle with his feet on the ground; the Father was sitting next to him but his feet did not touch earth. Behind them was the Spirit, a woman with long flowing silver-white hair, standing with a hand on each of their shoulders. It has stayed with me, touching something true inside.

Perhaps one of the most famous is Andrei Rublev's Trinity icon. In it, there are three figures seated at a table facing out towards the one who views them. It was painted around 1410, a time of great famine and death in Russia. The figures are of indeterminate gender. It is about hospitality, openness, welcoming and drawing all into sharing at the table. In the background, you can see Abram going to kill his best heifer and Sarai making bread. It was conceived as a sign of hope – that our God, the Trinity, is with us always, especially in harsh, demanding times. It reminds us that we are always being invited in to sit at the table with our God, to share in the feast that is served. But it is about the company – those who break the bread together in friendship and companionship – as much as it about what is eaten.

All these images seek to remind us that we are made in the image and likeness of God. Somehow we together as human beings reflect the Trinity and are meant to do so, ever more consciously. In the Gospel of Matthew, the very last lines mention the mystery and theology of the Trinity explicitly for the first time. Jesus commands his followers to go out into the whole world and first to make disciples from every land and nation and then to baptise them in the name of the Father and of the Son and of the Holy Spirit. Matthew's Gospel was written around 75–85 AD, and reflects the reality that this prayer was already a common occurrence and part of the ritual of Baptism in the Church. In this farewell, Jesus shares the authority and power that has been given to him by the Father in the ways of the Spirit with us. And it is given for imitation, making Christians, baptising them and teaching them, primarily by example. Christianity grew by leaps and bounds because people could see how Christians lived, not so much by any preaching or teaching but by example and the deeds and attitudes of small faith communities. Anything that we can say in regards to the Trinity, we must remember to try to incorporate into our own lives together in community and in the universal Church. This, of course, is not easy by any means.

Paul's letter to the Romans emphasises our place and relation to the Trinity. We are beloved children of God, gifted with the Spirit so that we can call God 'Abba', Father, with Jesus. This Spirit shared with us is one of freedom and intimacy, releasing us from fear, making us witnesses to Jesus' God for all to see and be drawn towards. Lastly, we are reminded that suffering is somehow a part of the Trinity as well as glory. But in all times, in all places, in all things, Jesus insists: 'I am with you all days until the end of time.' 'I am' – this is the name of God from the beginning in Exodus and it is the meaning of the name given to Jesus at the beginning in Matthew's Gospel: Emmanuel, meaning 'God is with us'. This line draws all of the Old Testament into Jesus' identity and power. With this confirmation of his power and presence we can live with the power of the Spirit to the glory of the Father, with Jesus. This is our meaning, our responsibility, our duty and blessing as we are invited deeper into the mystery of the Trinity.

QUESTIONS

1. When we think of the Trinity we are trying to get some sense of God and how we relate to this community of love, but we often forget or ignore the fact that all exists in God. On 31 October, 2011, the population of the world hit the seven billion mark and all these people are 'at home in God'. Whatever we learn about the Trinity we must connect to the entire human race and see all people as God sees them. How large is our heart and mind? Let us pray this week for all our lives to be stretched continually in our conception of God, but also in how to love everyone as God does.

2. There is no end to what we can know of God, how deeply we can attend to God, or to how much we can be known by God. God is limitless and there are no boundaries to how deeply we can dwell and abide with the Trinity. This is one of the many gifts of the Incarnation. What image comes to mind when you think of the Trinity? What does that image tell you about your place in God and in the world with all others?

The Body and Blood of Christ (Corpus Christi)

READINGS

EX 24:3-8; PS 116; HEB 9:11-15; MK 14:12-16, 22-26

> We cannot love God unless we love each other, and to love we must
> know each other. We know him in the breaking of the bread, and we
> are not alone any more. Heaven is a banquet and life is a banquet,
> too even with a crust, where there is companionship.
>
> DOROTHY DAY

> Lord Christ, we ask you to spread our tables with your mercy. And
> may you bless with your gentle hands the good things you have given
> us. We know that whatever we have comes from you. Thus whatever
> we eat, we should give thanks to you. And having received from your
> hands, let us give with equally generous hands to those who are poor,
> breaking bread and sharing our bread with them. For you have told
> us that whatever we give to the poor we give to you.
>
> ALCUIN OF YORK

With this Sunday we gather up the last of the mysteries of our religion.
There are three that are essential to our belief, our understanding of
who we are and how we are to live in the world in the power of God.
They are the Incarnation, the Resurrection and the Body of Christ –
both as Eucharist in the liturgy and the Church in the world, and as
the Trinity. All that we believe and profess are found in these mysteries.
Everything else in our religion is found under or in these realities.
And after this Sunday we will slide back into Ordinary Time for the
next six months! Half of the year we celebrate these great events that
we are part of and know in our own bodies and history, and half of
the year we seek to put them into practice, understand them more
deeply and live them out with grace, truth and power in the Church
for the world. The readings reflect the layered nature of this mystery
of the Body of Christ, first in its communal aspect and then in its more
individual experience.

Exodus tells us the story of the people agreeing to obey all of the law that has been given to them through Moses, and they celebrate their new sense of who they are as the people of God in a ritual. They take sacrifices of animals from each of the tribes and splash half of the blood over the altar. Then the covenant is read publicly. The people answer: 'All that the Lord has said, we will heed and do.' Moses then takes the other half of the blood in bowls and sprinkles it on the people. These words seal the covenant: 'This is the blood of the covenant which the Lord has made with you in accordance with all these words of his.' The words, the blood and the people are made one.

In Hebrews, we are told that Jesus is the only priest and that he has entered the sanctuary and passed over, shedding his own blood and handing over his life to God. There will be no more sacrifices because Jesus is the acceptable offering and he has taken us altogether into his own Body to be presented to God. Now when we gather, and bring bread and wine to the table, it is our lives, our sufferings and dyings that we bring with Jesus' own gift of himself to offer to the Father, to be made holy by the Spirit. What happens to the bread and wine, in being accepted by God, is what happens to all of us: we become the Body and Blood of Christ more deeply and truly. God accepts us always as he has taken Jesus at his word and in his life. Now the old sacrificial blood rituals have become more intimate, more demanding and more complete in Jesus' offering of himself and us to God in the Spirit.

The Gospel tells briefly of the Passover meal that Jesus celebrated with his friends and followers on the night before he died. Jesus follows the ancient ritual: taking the bread, blessing it and breaking it saying: 'This is my body.' He then takes the cup, gives thanks and passes it around to all of them, and when they have shared the cup, he says: 'This is my blood, the blood of the covenant, to be poured out on behalf of many."* The last line says that Jesus will not drink again of the fruit of the vine until the day when he drinks it new in the reign of God. We are given to drink of the wine of hope, of freedom and

---

* The actual meaning of this last word is 'all people'. Often a literal translation of a word, outside its context, distorts and contradicts its original meaning. Jesus' death and covenant is for all, not just for some of the people, some of the time.

joy, but Jesus as a human being – God-with-us – refrains until his reign comes in fullness among us all. Whatever our personal devotion to the Eucharist is, we must always remember that the word means giving thanks together, so it must draw us back to the community, to the Body of Christ throughout the world and through all time. This is the time to look at one another – the Body of Christ – with respect, delight, hope and love, knowing that if we are not the Body of Christ first, then what we celebrate in Church has little or no meaning. This is not first of all our personal time with Jesus, this is our communal embrace in which Jesus insists we be made more aware of one another, with him. Our God is a community, and we must return to this initial and foundational sense of the Body of Christ. We must come to be the presence of the Risen Lord in the world for all others to see, to come to know and become with us.

Jesus passed the bread and the cup around and we are to pass all that has been given to us in like manner. We are all in this together and are meant to receive the bread and cup from one another. As with the Trinity, it is a circle around the table in the company of Jesus where we share our stories, break bread, pool our resources and suffer, die and rise with Jesus as Lord, the host at the feast of freedom. Our God is a community and the Eucharist and liturgy must reflect that community ever more clearly so that others are drawn to the meal.

QUESTIONS

1. After this Sunday we will shift into Ordinary Time, or the Sundays after Pentecost, the time to embody in our own lives and our communities and parishes what we have experienced in these past seasons of the Church year. So much happens so quickly that we often don't absorb even a small portion of it. Take some time alone, and then with others in your small group, to reflect on what you want to study and pray over; practice and seek to incorporate these in your own life in these coming months. Delve into one of the mysteries, its season (they come mostly in groups of seven Sundays) and decide to do something that will reveal this love of God in your life. If you have trouble coming up with something, ask some of those you share the Word of God with weekly to help you out. And if you are not already in a group, join one that studies the Gospel weekly, following the Lectionary of the universal Church. Seek to make it come true in your own lives, in your place where you work, study, pray, worship and play to extend God's power and reign in the world.

2. There is a saying among many theologians that 'whatever we do in Church is practice for what we do outside'. The time we spend in Church in personal devotion and prayer must be translated into time we spend in the street and the world. Dom Hélder Câmara, who was Archbishop of Recife, Brazil, would speak and preach with great passion and tenderness about the 'Other Body of Christ': the poor and suffering. And he would remind his people that God cares more about how we treat this Other Body of Christ, the Other Eucharist, than any devotion we may have to what is in Church. How does this image of God among us affect you and your prayer life and practice, alone and with others in the Body of Christ?

Eleventh Sunday in Ordinary Time

READINGS

EZ 17:22-24; PS 92; 2 COR 5:6-10; MK 4:26-34

> The creation is not a study, a roughed-in sketch; it is supremely;
> meticulously created ... Even on the perfectly ordinary and clearly
> visible level, creation carries on with an intricacy unfathomable and
> apparently uncalled for.
>
> ANNIE DILLARD

> To create this new society, we must present outstretched and
> friendly hands, without hatred and rancour, even as we show great
> determination and never waver in the defence of truth and justice.
> Because we know that we cannot sow seeds with clenched fists. To
> sow we must open our hands.
>
> ADOLFO PÉREZ ESQUIVEL

This week we return to Ordinary Time. We move from all the marvellous mysteries that we have celebrated together ritually and turn to put them into practice in our lives and communities. We face almost six months of together seeking to make God's Word come true in our works and relationships, and choices. It is time to witness to, obey and attest to our belief so that others may be drawn into the Body of Christ and into God's kingdom.

The prophet Ezekiel looks to an image in nature, a tender shoot from the highest portion of a cedar tree that God will plant in Israel. It will flourish and grow and become a mighty cedar welcoming birds of every kind to come and dwell in its boughs and beneath its limbs. All the trees of the field will know that God brings down the great tree and lifts up the lowly one, withers what is green and makes the withered tree bloom. In reality, this is what has happened with all of us in these past months, in our Baptisms, Confirmations, Eucharists and moments of forgiveness and reconciliation. We are that great tree of life, hospitable to all the nations, to all peoples, especially those that need shelter, protection and care. We died and rose with Christ; the

Spirit has come upon us and now we are to be those who are lowly, yet blooming and welcoming others to new life.

This reading from Ezekiel is a more ancient rendering of the parable in today's Gospel: that of the mustard seed. In this parable, we return to Jesus' preaching of God's reign on earth. It is the sowing and planting, nurturing and sustaining of the revolution of 'lifting the lowly and bringing low the mighty'. It is preaching the Good News to the poor, who are the presence of God in our midst still. The kingdom, or 'kin-dom' as it is sometimes called now, is the place where God's power and authority rule relationships, making life ever more abundant for all, beginning with the least.

The mustard seed is a herb for seasoning and a weed that is small, seemingly inconsequential and, which once sown, grows quickly, spreads wildly and is nearly impossible to root out and stop once it takes hold in the ground. It shoots up, pushing out other plants, crowding them, becoming a bush, a shrub, sometimes a small tree, where the birds come to build their nests. The Word of God is the seed, but we too are the seed and the tree. We are to grow and live like the mustard seeds sown within our communities, offering shelter, shade, protection and a dwelling place for 'the birds'. The word used for these 'birds' is that of any common blackbird, of which there are hundreds of thousands, even millions everywhere! In the mustard weeds, in Jesus' communities, there is room for the least in the world and room for all sorts of creatures and peoples. Our hearts must expand like the seeds to be large enough to draw all in and welcome them home, here on earth.

We leap into this long Ordinary season of the Church and we will hear again Jesus' words, parables and images that call us to conversion, reflection, examination of our consciences; that call us to listen again and take Jesus' Word to heart. It is time once again for us to examine our lives, our communities, groups and parishes, to see if the life of God is present or if others are still keeping the birds from coming to nest among us. This half of the year is for growing, for shooting up and out into the world, drawing others into the great tree of life that is the Risen Lord among us.

QUESTIONS

1. Paul twice reminds us and our communities that we are courageous, and living with deep and wide hearts, as we seek to share what we have been given with others. Would people describe you, or your parish or small community, as courageous in welcoming and inviting others into the nurturing presence of the Tree of Life?

2. What does the Church in your diocese and in the world need to do this year to be welcoming, inviting, protecting and careful of the least among us? What actions and works might reveal the preaching of Jesus alive and with us? Is there a group of people who are looking for a place to settle and thrive, finding a home among Jesus' friends?

Twelfth Sunday in Ordinary Time

READINGS
JOB 38:1, 8-11; PS 107; 2 COR 5:14-17; MK 4:35-41

> Just as at sea those who are carried away from the direction of the
> harbour bring themselves back on course by a clear sign, such as a
> tall beacon light or a mountain peak coming into view, so Scripture
> may guide those adrift on the sea of life back into the harbour of
> the divine will.
>
> GREGORY OF NYSSA

> Lord, take me where you want me to go;
> Let me meet whom you want me to meet;
> Tell me what you want me to say;
> And keep me out of your way.
> Amen.
>
> FR MYCHAL JUDGE, OFM

In some ways, these first few weeks back into Ordinary Time and
practice draw us back to our foundations, so that we can start anew
with deepened awareness and fervour to live with each other as though
we were well-minted, yet newly baptised Christians. Today's reading
describing the storm that comes up quickly with surprising strength,
catching the boat with Jesus and the disciples in its fury, making them
cry out in fear, reminds us that life after Easter and all the great feasts
is definitely going to be full of surprises, unexpected turmoil and
moments of danger. But it is also clear that we must remember that
always, no matter what assails us and the Church and the world, Jesus
is with us in the boat. He is the strong, confident and the Risen One,
even if we perceive him to be asleep, unaware or not paying attention
to us. We must remember his presence, his Spirit, his Word among us,
and not be overcome by terror or get wrapped up in our own personal
needs of safety and security.

And we are reminded once again of a basic reality: we are all in
the same boat, whether in the Church, or on this planet earth; we are

all just human beings living out our lives spread out across the world. The Gospel begins with Jesus' suggestion: 'Let's cross over to the other side.' But it's prefaced with one of Mark's common phrases: on that day – any day, today, when evening draws on and the shadows fall, when the disciples and Jesus would have been worn out, tired and wanting to go home – Jesus initiates a move. Into the boats they go. And it is boats – this is the Church on the move towards the other side, out into Gentile territory, new vistas, new people to share the Good News with and draw into our company! Jesus is in the stern (every detail is important) and sound asleep. A squall blows up – wind, rain, waves, disorientation, rocking – and the boat starts taking on water. They panic, waking Jesus and complaining like children: 'Teacher, doesn't it matter to you that we're going to drown?'

We are called to remember that Jesus is more than Teacher. Jesus is the power of God in human flesh and all of the weather, the universe even, is subject to him and serves and protects those who accompany him. He stands face to the wind and sea and 'rebukes' them. This is another of Mark's favourite words in Jesus' mouth: he rebukes the man possessed in the synagogue (and he will later rebuke Peter) and it echoes Yahweh the God of the Israelites, who rebukes the sea during Exodus when the people are escaping Egypt (Psalm 106:9). He cries out: 'Be still. Be quiet.' Or more to the point: muzzle yourself. Get a grip. We must remember who this Jesus, who our teacher is: the beloved of God 'whom even wind and sea obey!' And so it begs the question: do we obey him? Do we listen to him and his words and take them to heart so that we are not lacking in faith, despairing and timid? We need both familiarity with Jesus and awe before him.

Along with Job we must be questioned about who we think our God is. In singing poetic images, Job is told to remember the creator's power and that even the processes and elements of creation are nothing in comparison to the power of God. There is no need to fear the powers of the sea, the air, or the earth, although in these days we must question ourselves about what we have done to the natural processes of the earth's ways to set them in turmoil.

Through our Baptism we claim now to live no longer for ourselves but for the sake of others and the God who made us all. Do we? We have to learn how to tap into the power flowing from Christ's resurrection, now in our own bodies and lives. We must rely on the power and presence of God among us, even if it appears from our vantage point that God is napping. We must remember we are a new creation! New things have come! Now the world is to stop in awe at the sight of us and what we do, as we grow in imitation of Jesus. We must make sure that the boat (the Church) is not acting like a timid whining child, but standing firm in rough seas (and we are in rough seas often), for our God is with us. And at the same time, perhaps we should start rocking some boats that need to be disturbed and brought back to shore.

QUESTIONS

1. The prayer at the beginning of this section is by Mychal Judge, a Franciscan priest who was chaplain to many in the fire and police departments in Manhattan, New York City. He died on 11 September 2001, and was carried out of one of the towers by his friends, some of the firemen that he served. Many think that he is a saint, meaning that his entire life was one of holiness, care for others, a radiance in ordinary things and in all days – many of which were filled with violence, loss, grief, accidents, death, suffering and all the experiences that life brings to us. His prayer is utterly simple and truthful. Pray it for a few days and think about what it means not to get in God's way.

2. Whenever we are in chaotic times, beset by trials, or find ourselves in unexpected, dangerous or violent situations, it is easy to forget that God is with us. But we can always go immediately to the Word of God in the Scriptures to find courage, hope and comfort. Read over the Gospel often this week and let God's Word seep deep into your mind and heart so that at night, you can sleep in peace with Jesus close by.

Thirteenth Sunday in Ordinary Time

READINGS

WIS 1:13-15, 2:23-24; PS 30; 2 COR 8:7, 9, 13-15; MK 5:21-43

> You who believe, and you who sometimes believe and sometimes
> don't believe much of anything, and you who would give almost
> anything to believe if only you could … 'Get up,' he says, 'all of you
> – all of you!'
>
> FREDERICK BUECHNER

> God entrusts the world to us. We are conduits of the vitality that
> keeps everything alive. In this way you may have the chance to wipe
> tears from the eyes of someone who will then know that they matter,
> that they are loved. This is Godly work.
>
> ARCHBISHOP DESMOND TUTU

The reading from Wisdom asserts strongly: 'God did not make death,
nor does he rejoice in the destruction of the living.' These words are
startling and shocking. There is so much death and all of us will die.
There is so much early death that is unnecessary through violence,
starvation, war, exile and lack of medical care. And yet our God is the
God of life. We have just celebrated the season when Christ destroyed
death in his dying and brought us unending life, yet we experience
suffering and death daily in our personal lives and in the news that
bombards us. This reality exists paradoxically alongside our belief that
we are made in the image of God and were made to be imperishable.
This is Wisdom for the beloved children of God.

In the Gospel, Jesus and the disciples get out of the boat on the
other side and walk into a world crowded with needy and desperate
people. The Gospel is long, a story that begins with a request and
then an interruption, but both impact one another and are meant to
be seen together. Jairus, a Jewish official, approaches Jesus and kneels
before him, begging for his daughter's life: 'please lay hands on her'.
Jesus immediately follows him towards his home. But the crowd is
pushing and shoving up against him, an image that vies with that of

Jesus 'going off' with Jairus – the phrase that indicates discipleship. And now comes the interruption. There is a woman who has been haemorrhaging, bleeding and slowly dying for twelve years! She is grasping at straws, has found no relief and exhausted her savings.

But she has heard about Jesus and manages, through the crowd, to come up behind him and reach out and touch his cloak – a fold, the fringes, an edge. She has to touch him, though in doing so she is risking everything and putting Jesus in an awkward position as well. She does non-verbally what Jairus does with words. Immediately (Mark's favourite word), the death in her stops and life courses through her again. Jesus is immediately conscious that his Spirit, his life, has been touched deeply – with diffidence, with need, and reverence, rather than in the way of the horde pushing against him. Someone drew him into their own soul. He stops and demands: 'Who touched my clothes?' In many more original translations it is simply: 'Who touched me?' Hemmed in by the crowd, there is one who sees him, knows him and moves intimately towards him, and Jesus responds in equal measure. The crowd, including his disciples, can't see who is in their midst – the giver of life, the Holy One of God – close enough to touch! He is looking for her now.

Desperation, suffering and closeness to death provide an open door for faith to enter in, for God to get in. Life must seek to fill up the spaces that death tries to wrest from it. The woman is fearful (fear is the beginning of wisdom) but she comes forward, and, like the official, falls to her knees and tells the whole truth of her story and her being bound now in life to Jesus. He calls her daughter and says that she is free of this illness (and how the touch of death was destroyed by touching the Body of Christ in her need). She is sent in peace to live.

And they continue on their way, and into the house of Jairus, where his twelve-year-old daughter, so ill, has died before they get to her. At only twelve years old, she lived as long as the woman who touched Jesus' cloak was dying. No need to trouble the teacher further. He may have words of life, but no power over death. They do not see him as Life itself. And Jesus counsels him – what he needs now is truth, like the woman who sought to touch him. He brings only Peter, James and

John and Jairus and his family with him – those who have made some sort of public commitment to him – while the professional mourners who made a living out of death try to overwhelm them with their cries. They mock him. He takes the child's hand and says: 'Taltitha, koum' – 'Little girl, get up.' Sometimes the power is in the words as they were spoken, rather than any translation. The little girl gets up! She starts walking around! Jesus tells them to give her something to eat. An ending that no one suspects! Eat at a time like this! But this is more than a healing, a bringing back to life. It is a Baptism, a confirming, and now it's time for feeding the new life that she and her family will live as followers of Jesus. Although the disciples still do not know it, this family recognise Jesus now as the Lord of Life, the Risen Lord, by his Word, his presence and his touch. Do we know him now as Life?

QUESTIONS

1. This story puts the questions to us: which side are we on? Are we with Jesus, but far from close to him, like the disciples? Are we on the far side of the lake, but still believers like Jairus and the woman who reached to touch his cloak? Are we ruled by death or by life?

2. There is suffering, long endurance and death in our world and we must face them – with Jesus. Sometimes there will be healing, through medical expertise, by changing our diets, our habits and way of life; sometimes by prayer, but we will have to face death eventually. Do we face it like the crowd, using it as a time to ridicule and mock life? Or do we face it together with the friends of God, seeking to obey Jesus' words? What is needed now is trust. What does it mean to trust in these difficult times?

All Saints

READINGS

REV 7:2-4, 9-14; PS 24; 1 JN 3:1-3; MT 5:1-12

> Heroes [and heroines] are those who kindle a great light in the world, who set up blazing torches in the dark streets of life for people to see by. Saints are those who walk through the dark paths of the world, themselves a light.
>
> FELIX ADLER

> All of the places of our lives are sanctuaries; some of them just happen to have steeples. And all of the people in our lives are saints; it is just that some of them have day jobs and will never have feast days named for them.
>
> ROBERT BENSON

Today we feast together with all those who have gone before us in faith – those we have known in our families, among our friends, in our neighbourhoods and across our lifetimes. This day reminds us that we are all saints! In the early Church, the followers of Jesus were referred to as 'the saints', so the letters were addressed to the saints in Jerusalem, the saints in Rome, the saints in Philadelphia (both then and now!) and so today it would be the saints in Nairobi, in Galway, in Chicago, in Mumbai, in Kyoto, etc. Whenever John calls his community 'Beloved', it is another way of calling them saints, the holy ones of God, the children of God, and that's who we are today! What we will be like one day hasn't been revealed yet, but we are told that we will be 'like God, for we shall see him as he is'. This is our hope. This is what we stake our lives on day to day. And so today we remember all the saints, especially those whom we know were holy, and who struggled in their lives and in their worlds to be the children of God, living their lives as gifts and offerings to God. Most of them are icons and saints to be imitated, incorporating their insights and experiences, their stories and even their failings into our own lives now.

The Gospel looks at the crowds and the great multitude 'which no one can count from every nation, race, people and tongue' who lived the beatitudes and were blessings for others while they were in the world. They were the poor in spirit who lived in solidarity with those who lived without the basic necessities of life, who lived hoping for a dearer life and shared with them from the gifts God has given to them. They were those who mourned, and lived in solidarity with those who knew war, violence, terror, displacement, homelessness and needless suffering. They prayed with them and for them and sought to comfort them, sometimes even in their own grief. They were the ones who were meek and non-violent and who lived without harming others or the earth, who lived close to the earth, humble and aware of their place with others as God's poor – those sometimes called 'the salt of the earth' in society.

They were the ones who taught us to hunger and thirst for justice, for holiness and righteousness, like we hunger for food, for water, for acceptance and love. They wanted life ever more abundant for everyone. They were the ones who knew Mercy as their God and who turned in mercy towards others with forgiveness, with reconciliation and communion, hard as it was, day after day. They were the ones who lived single-heartedly – their priorities, like God's, the coming of the reign of justice, peace and freedom – and we could see a glimpse of God reflected in their eyes. They were the ones who worked tirelessly for peace, for no war, for harmony in communities, parishes and among families, and between husbands and wives, seeking to make friends of enemies. And they were the ones often persecuted, rejected, shunted aside not only by members of their families, but members of society and sometimes even by Church.

And they knew how to rejoice, in spite of everything, to laugh, to sing, to bless God and give praise and in all things to be grateful for life, and all that life entails – distress, struggle, failures, and long faithfulness. They were the company we kept, and those who were our teachers, godparents, friends, co-workers, family, acquaintances, sometimes people who lived in the same decade or somewhere else in the world who we'd heard of, met once or never even knew. They were all saints and we, the saints living today, hang onto their coattails and grasp hold of their memories and look at their pictures and tell stories of them, because they're home free and are rooting for us to come and join them. They're waiting for us, praying and hoping that we do marvellous things for the earth and all the children of God in our day, and in our place. Today is one great feast of all the unknown, uncanonised, unheralded, unsung folk who were truly saints and truly known to God. For us, they were marked with the seal of God's delight, and shone like the stars of night as they shone for moments in our lives and the lives of many others. They encourage us to be what we are called to be, what God dreams us to be – saints – and some day, who knows what we will all be like, seeing God as God is.

QUESTIONS

1. Dorothy Day, the founder of the Catholic Worker, who lived and treated the poor, the street folk, immigrants and beggars with utmost dignity, once told her friends, much to their surprise, not to attempt to have her canonised. She wanted to be just one of 'them', known and loved by 'them' and to be one of the great multitude of the Body of Christ. What does her wanting to disappear into the Body of Christ say to you about your life?

2. We are all the saints of God. As you live your life, what would you like to be remembered as by your friends, family and others? Would you like to be the patron of computer programmers, tweeters, or guitar players, catechists? What would you choose and why?

3. Who in your personal experience was truly a saint, because you knew that in their presence you were close to a friend of God? Share a story or two about them. Do you think of yourself as a friend of God, a saint?

Fourteenth Sunday in Ordinary Time

READINGS

EZ 2:2-5; PS 123; 2 COR 12:7-10; MK 6:1-6

> Of all people, Christians are the most blunt and relentless realists. They are free to face the world as it is without flinching, without shock, without fear, without surprise, without embarrassment, without sentimentality, without guile or disguise. They are free to live in the world as it is.
>
> WILLIAM STRINGFELLOW

Today's readings are blunt, realistic and confrontational. They are about prophets in our midst, driven by the power of the Spirit and Word of God to get our attention and speak a word of truth to us, whether we hear it and take it to heart or not. First we hear of the prophet Ezekiel, addressed as 'Son of Man', one who comes from the people and yet is sent to the people by God. He is told that those he is sent to are 'rebels who have revolted against God like their ancestors, and they are hard of face and obstinate of heart.' This is not going to be an easy task but that does not stop God from making sure they know that a prophet has been among them. Whether or not they take heed or resist, God's Word will be proclaimed.

And this is the set up for the Gospel. Jesus goes home and to the synagogue on the Sabbath, as is his custom, and begins to preach the Word of God and the reign and power of God in the world to his own kin and neighbours, as he has been doing elsewhere. They are astonished, disbelieving, mocking, resistant, and take offence at him. Not a great reception by any standards. And Jesus' reaction is one of sadness, shock and dismay at their utter lack of faith in his words and in him. And so, their disdain blocks Jesus' ability to perform any mighty deeds among them, except to cure a few people by laying hands on them. For Jesus it is a stunning disappointment and will be a turning point in his ministry and in his sense of who he is. It is the beginning of outright rejection by practically everyone in his own religious community, eventually even by his own disciples.

Jesus sees himself as a prophet and, like the prophets before him, he is without honour in his own place, among his own people. They see him as they have known him before Baptism, before the descent of the Spirit upon him, before God's proclamation of him as his beloved servant and child who brings him delight in his words and deeds. They know him, he is just like them, they know his brothers and sisters, his mother and father. There is no way he can be possessed of such wisdom, grace and power. This thinking will be the reaction of many of his own religion and so Jesus knows scorn, humiliation and a refusal to see who he is.

Paul identifies with the experience of scorn in his own life, describing the insults, hardships, persecutions and constraints that are part and parcel of his daily life. They co-exist with the power of Christ that dwells within him. In his case, as in ours, there are also weaknesses, failures and personal foibles to contend with. But, like Paul, we have the grace of God to strengthen our attempts to share God's hopes for us all with others.

It is hard to accept that many of the people we want most to share the Word of God with will not accept what we have to say. Perhaps because of our pasts, and their assumptions about us, they think that there is no way that such wisdom and truth would be given to us. These are the first steps in knowing in our own flesh and relationships what finding power in weakness may entail. But we are free as the beloved brothers and sisters of Jesus, the children of God and the witnesses of the Spirit of Life and Truth to face all that people can do to us without flinching, knowing that our reality is stronger and more free than anything society and its institutions can dish out to us. We can and will prevail and the Spirit sends us out anyway. The Word is to be preached whether it is heeded or not.

QUESTIONS

1. Those closest to Jesus cause him the deepest distress – his family, neighbours, those he grew up with – and it shocks and saddens him. He had hopes that they would rejoice in what he had to share with them. In your own life and relationships, are there certain people, with whom you want to share what is most precious to you, and yet they don't want it – or worse they don't want it from you? Have you ever thought to share that sorrow with Jesus who knew it in his own life too?

2. These were people that Jesus worshipped with daily and on the Sabbath. Is this the experience within your own communities, a Church that doesn't listen or heed the Word and the Spirit given in Baptism and Confirmation to its own members?

3. Paul has a 'thorn in his flesh', a weakness that is glaringly apparent to him and to all around him. He has just one! Sometimes we can feel like we have a whole bush of thorns! What are some of the thorns that you think hinder you from bringing the Good News of God's forgiveness, love, justice and mercy to others?

4. Do you ever wonder if you are acting like Jesus' family and neighbours – rejecting out of hand those around you who you think you know, thinking that God certainly doesn't use them to speak the truth in power? Who do you refuse to listen to because of your past experience of them?

Fifteenth Sunday in Ordinary Time

READINGS
AMOS 7:12-15; PS 85; EPH 1:3-14; MK 6:7-13

> Those who want to bear the mark of the Spirit and the fire that Christ baptises with must take the risk of renouncing everything and seeking only God's reign and justice.
>
> ARCHBISHOP OSCAR ROMERO

> Go forth in peace, for you have followed the good road. Go forth without fear, for he who created you has made you holy, has always protected you, and loves you as a mother. Blessed be you, my God, for having created me.
>
> CLARE OF ASSISI

Last week we saw what the fate of the prophet could be in Jesus' hometown synagogue, and now we are being sent off two by two as a company of prophets following in Jesus' own footsteps proclaiming the Gospel. We are given authority to discern what is good and evil and to anoint with oil those who are sick. We are to bring strength and enduring grace to those who are ill, burdened and struggling whether they are cured or not. This exhortation is very pragmatic and practical, like a guide on how to pack for a journey where the journey itself is more crucial than the destination! In the very first chapter of Mark, we, his disciples, were summoned from our jobs and livelihoods to catch fish, to hook folk who would come along in Jesus' company and share in the Good News of God. Now we see how we are to go on our way.

They go two by two. Often, in the past, this was interpreted as two of the disciples – all men. But the twelve disciples are not just those named, they are the model for all followers of Jesus. More recently it has come to be understood that whole families travelled with Jesus, and that two by two could be husband and wife, two friends, men and/ or women. All that we do, no matter our vocation, we are to do with others. This is part and parcel of our lives whether we are married, single, belonging to a community – we are all sent out. It can be a lifelong commitment, or it can be a year or two, a portion of a year, two weeks when we can work with others. We don't have to go far – even our own neighbourhood is often far enough – but we are to share our belief, our practice and the understanding and freedom that has been given to us in some personal way.

The practices of what to bring might seem strange to us but they reveal Jesus' priorities: take a walking stick and go no farther than a day's distance – eight to ten miles around our own neighbourhood. Wear sandals, probably good sturdy ones for whatever the terrain might be. You don't need change of clothes, no food and no money, this way no one will be inclined to rob you and your journey will be one of peace and connections. Look for someone to host you, take you in and feed you, give you a bit of rest from your journey and a place to work from, even meet with others there. Preach repentance – change of heart, change of mind, change of lifestyle and change of priorities. This preaching can be other than words, it can be work shared, the kingdom made present in all the ways people need hope, help and presence. Build a house, a school, dig a trench, lay pipes for water, teach another language. You could make and serve food to the hungry, run a dispensary for medicines, bring food or supplies for a school, give clothes, provide medical services, help people write resumes. The possibilities are endless. Stay where you settle, don't go looking around for a better place. And when your presence, your words and work are not appreciated by some, don't say anything against them – shake the dust from your sandals and go home.

These suggestions may seem strange and odd to us, but it is an admonition for anyone who seeks to preach or share the Gospel in any way to rely on the hospitality of those we go to, and on their already open and generous hearts. We have to remember that to go as prophets is to go to those who already believe, but who need depth, breadth and a encouragement to extend that faith into practice. A prophet is interested in God's priorities: what constitutes true worship, the care of the poor and the coming of justice and peace. For us, these sound like three very separate things, but for prophets, and for God, they are all one. What constitutes true worship of God is care for the poor, which brings God's kingdom where there is justice and abiding peace and that is the only worship God wants. And so the call to repentance, to healing and to driving out demons involves working for justice, for peace, doing the corporal works of mercy and building the kingdom where its walls might be breached and its foundation sagging.

People will react to us as they did to the prophet Amos – go home, leave us alone, get a job, live with the way things are – and we must remember that we, along with Amos, are called by God to be an alternative of hope and possibility for others, whether it makes people uncomfortable or calls them to come and work with us for God's way in the world. When we do this kind of work, we must travel light and be ready to move on, without rancour or condemnation. This way of living isn't for everyone and not always for a long time, but it is for all of us at some time and for some a distinct call that is a proclamation in itself. If it is specifically for the Twelve it is clear that all leadership needs to be called to conversion, along with the larger Church.

QUESTIONS

1. The reading from Ephesians is a long prayer of praise and thanksgiving, blessing God as Father, in Jesus, with the Spirit, for all the blessings he has given to us. We have so many blessings given for all time: forgiveness, faith, grace, being God's beloveds, being chosen to share his work in the world with others. God has lavished us with wisdom, with the Spirit, with hope and the word of truth. We so often take all of these for granted. Perhaps this week, end each day with your own litany of thanksgiving for all that God has given you.

2. After thanksgiving and praise, the best way to give thanks is to share that with others. We are told that this is the first instalment of what God is giving to us –we can't just keep taking, we need to pass it along. Who can you do this with two by two or in small groups? Who needs something of what God has lavished on you?

Sixteenth Sunday in Ordinary Time

READINGS

JER 23:1-6; PS 23; EPH 2:13-18; MK 6:30-34

> A Gospel that doesn't unsettle, a word of God that doesn't get under anyone's skin, a word of God that doesn't touch the real sin of the society in which it is being proclaimed, what Gospel is that?
>
> ARCHBISHOP OSCAR ROMERO

> O God, whose son Jesus Christ cared for the welfare of everyone and went about doing good to all: Grant us the imagination and the perseverance to create in this country and through the world a just and loving society for the human family; and make us agents of your compassion to the suffering, the persecuted, and the oppressed, through the Spirit of your son, who shared our human sufferings, Jesus Christ. Amen.
>
> FROM NORWICH CATHEDRAL

Each Sunday we are being introduced to another prophet and to Jesus' prophetic Word and actions, inviting us to follow him and to be prophetic in our communities, society and Church today. The reading from Jeremiah is an especially powerful and provocative one and is supposed to be read in contrast to Psalm 23. The Word of the Lord is woe to bad shepherds who scatter the sheep and mislead them, even drive them away. There has been no care for them but instead they have known evil from their leaders and they live in fear of them, wondering what they will do to them next. And the Word of the Lord declares that God will come and gather the flock back together, nurturing them, feeding them, making sure that they flourish, increase and know peace. And one day there will be One who is a righteous shoot to David (once a shepherd) who will bring justice and wisdom to all who dwell in the land. In fact, his name will be 'The Lord our Justice'. Jeremiah was dealing with the leadership of the king, officials, priests and false prophets who told the people what the leaders wanted them to hear. Sadly, at times, some sheep are still dealt with shabbily and not listened to, while many in the larger Church are disheartened by the decisions and practices of some in positions of leadership.

In the Gospel, the apostles gather back with Jesus after their short forays out to preach, teach and do the work of the Gospel – healing, curing and sharing God's power on earth with others hungry to hear it. Jesus draws them away to rest but they are followed by great crowds of people. Even when they get in the boat, the people walk on foot around the lake to get to them and arrive before they do. What is left out in Mark's Gospel, just prior to this reading, is the gruesome detailed murder of John the Baptist. The people are distraught, fearful of what is going to happen next, for their prophet who spoke the truth to their own leaders, Jews like themselves, has been butchered at a dinner party. The apostles want time alone with Jesus but as soon as Jesus sees the numbers of people and their terror and despair, their abject needs, he leaves the apostles and goes to them. Jesus sees and his heart is moved to pity.* He sees himself as a good shepherd entrusted with all these sheep and he moves to be with them – to protect them, nurture them, let his presence comfort them and keep them together, safe and at home with him.

In essence, Jesus does what the letter to the Ephesians describes. He brings us all close to each other and to God in himself and breaks down the walls of hate, fear and enmity, and abolishes all laws and enforcement of them that causes pain, separation, exile and division. He brings peace with his presence. He not only preaches peace in the midst of violence and hate, he draws near those scattered and driven away and gathers us all into the presence and dwelling place of God. Whatever the apostles experience, they are to look to him and model their lives on how he is moved to pity and anger at the injustice, violence and horror that his people must live with. They must stop everything they are doing to make sure the community is one, gathered, taught, given peace, a sense of belonging, and the Word

---

* The phrase 'moved to pity' has two meanings in the Gospel, and here it carries both: to prompt a physical reaction to what one witnesses (for example, throwing up) and to feel such anger towards what you see that you give birth to something new and unimagined. Jesus' reactions are this strong and he moves to a new level of intensity in his peaching and teaching.

of God. Though Jesus does not say it here (he does in other places), he is telling them that he will not tolerate them doing anything other than what he himself does for his people, that is, making them one, establishing peace and reconciling them all with God into his one Body, through the Cross. He is willing, and they must be, to suffer so that they do not become bad shepherds.

QUESTIONS

1. The Scriptures tell the truth about everyone and are especially important for anyone who has a role of power, authority and leadership in the Church. If you could write a letter to your shepherds, using the words of today's readings, what would you say to them?

2. The letter to the Ephesians talks about those who are far off and those who are near, and that in Jesus' cross and death and resurrection we are all reconciled to each other and God. Who are those still afar off in our Church that we need to draw near to so that the peace that Jesus preached might be a reality among us? What can we do to help gather us more together in the peace of Christ?

Seventeenth Sunday in Ordinary Time

READINGS
2 KGS 4:42-44; PS 145; EPH 4:1-6; JN 6:1-15

> At this table we put aside every worldly separation based on culture,
> class or other differences. This communion is why all prejudice,
> all racism, all sexism, all deference to wealth and power must be
> banished from our parishes, our homes and our lives.
>
> JOSEPH CARDINAL BERNARDIN

> Charity depends on the vicissitudes of whim and personal wealth;
> justice depends on commitment instead of circumstance. Faith-based
> charity provides crumbs from the table; faith-based justice offers a
> place at the table.
>
> BILL MOYERS

This Sunday, we return to John's Gospel and we will stay with chapter
six of John's gospel for the next five weeks. We will begin with Jesus
feeding the crowd, an act that sets the pattern and tone for all that
follows. John's account of feeding the crowd that numbers about five
thousand men contains a number of important details that differ from
the other Gospel accounts of this event. If there are five thousand
men, then according to those who count crowds, the ratio of women
and children to men is usually about five or six to one, which means
the crowd numbers around twenty-five to thirty thousand. And it is
close to the celebration of the Passover ritual, the feast of freedom
and liberation from bondage and slavery which is the heart of the
Jewish liturgical year. It is the feast that makes a throng of disparate
tribes into the people that belong to God. The reason for the feeding
is the long time they have spent with Jesus and the healing and care
of the sick (which is always a sign of the presence of God among the
people). It is a meal of survival and need, a feast (there is so much left
over) and it is Eucharist (the word for leftovers or fragments is the
word used for the bread of the table at liturgy). Again and again, the
vastness and the number of the people are emphasised.

Elisha's servant in the first reading is told to give twenty barley loaves to over one hundred people. Barley loaves were the bread of the poor. And when he objects, he is told: do it and there will be leftovers. In the Gospel, Jesus questions Philip about where they can find food to feed so many. Philip is overwhelmed. Even if they had money worth two thirds of a year's wages, they couldn't even begin to feed them. But Andrew offers a bit of information: there is a young child with five barley loaves and two fish – this was probably his whole family, friends and neighbours' meal being offered to Jesus. The catalyst comes from a child, or the child's mother who would have made the loaves, or perhaps the father who caught or bought the fish. Jesus ordered that all the men sit down on the grass to be served and made clear that all were welcome to eat as much as they wanted.

There are echoes of manna in the desert of the Exodus as the people are brought to freedom and the prophet feeds the poor and hungry with the offerings meant for God. Jesus gives thanks and gives it all away. Jesus is the shepherd feeding his sheep in good pasture and making sure all have enough. This is a feast born of pity and compassion for the majority who are without the basic necessities of life. This is the bread of justice, and the bread of peace. And what is the sign? Jesus initiates the sharing, but it seems someone, a child from the crowd, brings what his family has before Jesus asks for it. The gesture and ritual are simple: the gifts are accepted from the young child, on behalf of the people. And Jesus distributes it and it passes among the people. It is up to the disciples to collect the leftovers.

It is a marvellous thing to behold – a miracle – this sharing among all believers and those who are curious, sceptical, hungry, seeking, needing across all divides of economics, nationalities, classes of people, races and position in society and religion. And this is Eucharist, the Body of Christ given to us in teaching, in healing, in filling our deepest needs, physically and in mind, heart and soul. So it is also mystery. What happened that day, and on all days, when the crowds were fed and all had enough and barriers were breached? What happens every time we gather for Eucharist – or what should happen among us? What takes place breaks open political and economical issues and reveals injustice and violence for what it is, making it personal – those we eat with, pray with, and live our lives with in Jesus' presence. No matter how much we reveal of the mystery, there will be more to say about the generosity and the depth of love our God has for us in the giving of the Bread of Life – the Body of Christ – to us as food, as hope, as passion for the possible, for sharing, for freedom, for friendship and intimacy, for justice and peace for all – especially in the shadow of religious and social violence in collusion with one another.

Over the coming weeks, we will feed on this Word of God, this experience of the feeding of the masses of people, this image of God shepherding us and making us one in communion, feeding us with himself in so many ways. It is time for a long, drawn-out reflection on this mystery of God-with-us and God as our food, our sustenance, our grace, Spirit and life together.

QUESTIONS

1. A young child brings his family and friends' food to Andrew. Children know when they are hungry and, no matter what else is going on, it's time to eat. Families had followed Jesus and others around the lake, bringing their sick and elderly with them, and bringing food with them. It is offered as gift. Someone has been listening to the teaching of Jesus and makes a move. Someone is thinking like Jesus. When you gather with others, are you ever the one who sees the need and makes the first move to make sure everyone gets what they need, whether that be food, clothing, water, housing or medical care?

2. When you come to church, education classes, prayer services or liturgy and there is food served, who goes home with the leftovers? When you study the Word of God in the Scriptures, what do you do with the leftovers – all the extra therein that is given along with what you need?

Eighteenth Sunday in Ordinary Time

READINGS

EX 16:2-4, 12-15; PS 78; EPH 4:17, 20-24; JN 6:24-35

> The question of bread for myself is a material question, but the question of bread for my neighbour is a spiritual question.
>
> NIKOLAI BORDYAEV

> I don't preach a social Gospel; I preach the Gospel, period. The Gospel of our Lord Jesus Christ is concerned for the whole person. When people were hungry, Jesus didn't say, 'Now is that political or social?' He said, 'I feed you.' Because the good news to a hungry person is bread.
>
> ARCHBISHOP DESMOND TUTU

At the end of last Sunday's Gospel, the people reacted to being fed and had all they wanted by deciding to make Jesus their king. Some thought he was the prophet that was to come, the presence of God's justice and peace with the people, perhaps the Messiah or one long awaited, like Moses. And as soon as that is even hinted at, Jesus leaves. He is not who they think he is, and he most surely is not who they want him to be. And this whole chapter of John is trying to say things about who Jesus is, often using images from Exodus and the earlier traditions, but always hinting at more that cannot easily be said or explained. In a sense we will only have fragments, pieces of the awesomeness, holiness, depth and sense of who God is in Jesus. Today Jesus calls himself the gift of the Father and the bread of life.

The reading from Exodus reveals how little the people understood that they were being drawn out of slavery into a land and a life of promise, hope and abundance. They get bound up in day-to-day survival and can think only about food. And so God feeds them, so that they can begin to learn to trust in God. They are fed strange food – manna, the meaning of which is 'what is this?'. Moses tells them: this is the bread that the Lord has given you to eat. It sustains them daily, but it is also meant to feed their desire for freedom, right living and the worship of their God.

Jesus is feeding us food: barley loaves, torn apart and shared is meant to satisfy our bodily hunger and at the same time to feed our hunger for God, for wisdom, for freedom as the children of God. And in light of all these hungers, it is also the Eucharist, the bread of thanksgiving for all God has done for us in Jesus' life, death and resurrection.

Jesus begins by telling us that he is trying to give us food that endures. The last line is supposed to hang with us, echo over and over inside us and make us wonder and hunger for Jesus' relationship with the Father: 'I am the bread of life; whoever comes to me will never hunger, and whoever believes in me will never thirst.' In the wisdom tradition of the Jews, the Word of the Scripture is this well of water that slakes thirst and this bread/manna that makes us hunger for holiness, justice and truth – in a word, God. And this is what Jesus wants to give us: God as food, in bread for sustenance shared together, but also in Scripture – his flesh among us in Word, and in his presence among us in the Body, especially in those who hunger always.

Our ancestors ate the bread of heaven daily and did not understand what they were eating. When we eat the bread of life we sometimes do not understand what we are eating either. Jesus is the food and life-blood of God and is given to us daily in the Word, in bread and wine, in community, in sacrifice and in the cross in the world. Do we see and understand, or are we like those at the time of Jesus? Are we blind, selfish, resistant, uncomprehending and unbelieving because we want material signs? Do we want our material needs taken care of as a sign that God cares about us, rather than learning to hunger and thirst for justice for all, bread for all, and wholeness for the earth?

QUESTIONS

1. In today's economic and financial climate of insecurity, do you spend a lot of time thinking and praying for your 'daily bread', your future security and the material needs of yourself and your family? Do you want material signs from God that you're loved and taken care of, rather than seeking to share with others, even in your lack, and looking to Jesus to feed you hope, freedom, joy and daily trust so that you can do the work of the kingdom in all times?

2. D. T. Niles said: 'Christianity is one beggar telling another beggar where he found bread.' With whom do you share the bread of life, the wisdom and the Word of God in the Scriptures that makes you hungry for the things and the works of God?

3. We are hungry for more than food. What kinds of things do you hunger for that are just as crucial to survival as food? Where do you go looking for these things? Do you look for them with others, or just on your own?

Nineteenth Sunday in Ordinary Time

READINGS
1 KGS 19:4-8; PS 34; EPH 4:30–5:2; JN 6:41-51

> What we know of the world comes to us primarily through vision.
> Our eyes, however, are sensitive only to that segment of the spectrum
> located between red and violet; the remaining 95 per cent of all
> existing light (cosmic, infrared, ultraviolet, gammas, and x-rays)
> we cannot see. This means that we only perceive 5 per cent of the
> 'real' world.
>
> AMOS VOGEL

> Lord, impart to us the meaning of the words of Scripture and the
> light to understand it.
>
> HILARY OF POITERS

By this point in preaching and listening to the Word of the Lord in
John 6, everyone needs some simple prayer to be enlightened, and
to understand, step back and to remind ourselves that what we are
trying to delve deeply into is mystery – the mystery of our God that
goes beyond our imaginations, gives the Beloved, the Word made flesh
as food to all. We are being told that we feed on God, that God lives,
abides and sustains us, and becomes our flesh in bread and wine and
word. God in Jesus wants to inhabit our bodies, and use our flesh in
the world and share in our daily lives, as we come together to eat and
drink to our life and resurrection.

Our resurrection lives began at Baptism. We don't wait until we
die to begin to live this newness. We were sealed in the Spirit, forgiven
and made beloved children along with Jesus. We dwell in God and
God in us and so our lives are supposed to reveal that in our behaviour
towards one another. Always, we are seeking to love as Christ has loved
us and to give ourselves over as Jesus gave himself for our life. That
is to please God always. The mystery of what Jesus is trying to tell us
feeds us courage and hope, passion for holiness, justice and truth and
graceful living in the midst of everything around us.

The reading from Kings tells the end of the story of Elijah, who has challenged the false prophets of Baal and the Queen and is now running for his life. After a day in the desert he just wants to lay down and die, but that will not be allowed. He is fed for his journey with a hearth cake and a jug of water. He wants to sleep after eating and he is awakened again – it is time to get up and go. He eats again, and on the strength of that food he walks forty days and nights to the mountain of God. Now, if Elijah can do that on a hearth cake from God, what can we do when fed with the bread of life? We are told by Jesus in today's Gospel: 'whoever eats this bread will live forever; and the bread that I will give is my flesh for the life of the world'. We have been initiated into a new way of life and it is this bread of Jesus, Word and flesh that feeds that life now and until forever.

Elijah murmurs and complains and the crowd listening to Jesus murmurs and complains. Both are steeped in their own illusions, wants and lack of perception. They see only the superficial once again: Jesus' family origins, who his parents were. They refuse to see that who is standing before them has been sent by the Father into the world and is trying to get them to see God! If only they could see that he is the bread that feeds eternal life in us, he is what gives them the strength to believe, to not succumb to despair, violence or hopelessness and to stake their life on God's word and God's promises that are beyond anything they could dare to imagine. They resist. They fix on what they think they know about God, their tradition, and they are ignorant, narrow-minded and hard-hearted. Jesus tries to remind them of a piece of their ancient tradition from the prophet Jeremiah: that they shall all be taught by God. He is trying to teach them about the Father and about his own life in God. He is trying to tell them that this life is stronger than any power, stronger than any death.

It is too much and they will have nothing to do with him. They are thick-headed, stubborn and won't let Jesus' words or presence, or even his works, stretch their image of God's love. This is the mystery of the Incarnation (God become flesh, dwelling among us) and the mystery of the Eucharist (God become flesh dwelling in us and feeding us on word and bread and wine). This is an amazing truth about God, but it is an amazing truth about us as well. God is our sustenance, our very breath and life, but we too are the Body of Christ by Baptism, water and illumination. We become what we eat and together we are the Bread of Life for others, as Jesus' Word and Flesh is for us. It is hard to comprehend God's graciousness to us and hard to accept that we are now God's presence in the world, and that the honour we give to the Bread and Wine – the Body and Blood of Jesus – is also the honour and reverence we are now commanded to give to the Body of Christ in the world of all flesh.

QUESTIONS

1. The opening line of this reading from Ephesians is startling: 'Brothers and sisters: Do not grieve the Holy Spirit of God.' In Baptism and Confirmation we were made the dwelling place of God and we are to look on one another and treat one another with kindness, forgiveness, mercy and compassion. We are not to revile one another, or shout in anger or hold grudges and be bitter towards one another. How do we grieve the Holy Spirit of God in our parishes and churches today? How can we instead imitate Christ in our daily encounters with one another?

2. We are the Body of Christ. We feed on the Body of Christ and we are sustained by the Body of Christ. We go forth into the world to draw others to look at their deepest hungers and draw them to this sustaining Word of God and Eucharist so they can share in this mystery. Do we reflect upon and seek to live our lives for the life of the world? This is what Eucharist is given to us for – to share it and bring life to the world. How can you and others do this after feeding on the bread of everlasting life?

3. Elijah complains, and so do the people Jesus is trying to teach. Do we complain and refuse to struggle with the depth of God's great mysteries?

The Assumption of the Blessed Virgin Mary

READINGS

REV 11:19A, 12:1-6A, 10AB; PS 45; 1 COR 15:20-27; LK 1:39-56

> Mary speaks for all those who have been lowly, on the outside, at the bottom, colonised, suppressed, and totally outside of the halls of princes and power wielders.
>
> SIDNEY CALLAHAN

> Now in the deep womb of the Sacred Word I will search for myself, Spirit and Truth.
>
> BERNARD OF CLAIRVAUX

This feast of Mary is also known as the Falling Asleep of the Mother of God in the Orthodox Church, and it is celebrated with a mixture of lamentation and rejoicing. As with all feasts of Mary, we are drawn towards God through the experiences of her life, and in this case, her death and the promise shared with all of us in Christ's resurrection from the dead. In some sense, it is all about Jesus, the Father and the Spirit, and we must look at this feast as pointing to the mystery of the resurrection. First we believe that God the Father raised Jesus from the dead in the power of the Spirit. Then we believe that the Father will raise all of us from the dead, with Jesus, in the power of the Spirit, that one day all will know the fullness of resurrection life at the end of time when 'Christ the Risen One hands over the kingdom to his God and Father and he has destroyed every sovereignty and every authority and power.' Most importantly, we believe that our resurrection begins in Baptism and that our lives are practice for the coming fullness that one day we will all experience, with Christ, with Mary and with all those who have gone before us in faith.

And so the Gospel reading reminds us of how we are to live this resurrection life, ever more fully here and now in the world with the hope of its completion one day. It is the story of Mary travelling to visit her cousin Elizabeth. Mary's greeting of 'shalom' – peace be with you – stirs the Spirit in Elizabeth, and her baby, John, leaps in joy at the sound of the voice of the mother of the One he is to herald. In a sense, this is Mary's confirmation by the Spirit in Elizabeth as she cries out, as prophets do, acknowledging Mary's act of faith and believing the Word of the Lord that came to her. It is a small Church gathering of two pregnant women and their children yet to be born, standing on a hillside proclaiming that the Good News is loose in the world, though hardly anyone knows it yet. Elizabeth blesses Mary, but she blesses all those who believe in the Word that is spoken to them – and today that is all of us.

Mary responds with a singing soul, in exaltation of God who does such great things for all people and for her personally. It is a psalm gleaned from many experiences and prayers of the books of the Old Testament. And it is always about God, not about her. It is about God as Saviour, as the one who sets all Israel and all peoples free, for life ever more abundantly. It is about the Almighty whose deeds are never ending. It is about the history of her people and the foundation of God's intervention in the world since the beginnings of creation. She sings of the Exodus, and the people being drawn out of bondage into the promised land of freedom.

Mary, as a prophet, cries out the three revolutions that are already in motion in the world because of her Child, the Beloved of God. The first revolution is where the proud are scattered and their conceit is shattered, beginning with each person, but especially with those who scorn God or use religion to serve their own ends – it implies a revolution of the person. The second revolution involves the casting down of the high and mighty, the rulers and powers of society that live off the backs of the lowly and the poor – a revolution of politics. The third revolution turns to the hungry, filling them with good things – food, water, justice, hope, peace and forgiveness – and sends those who are rich away empty. It is the revolution of economics and survival so that there is abundant life, beginning with those who need it the most. Mary sings of the prophets' promises and her Child's very Word, Presence, Body and Being.

Mary stays three months with Elizabeth, learning from her what it will mean to bear a child in the world, knowing the support and companionship of an older woman during the first months of her pregnancy and the last ones of Elizabeth's. She dwells with the Word taking hold of her flesh and she searches for her own spirit and truth in her Child. This is what we are reminded to do as well on this day– to dwell with the Word that Mary gave birth to and let it seep into our flesh, so that we too search for our own spirit and our own truth in the Word as she did. Now the Word affords us a deep womb, where we can become the beloved children of God and give birth to God's will and kingdom in our world.

Mary now enjoys the fullness of God's presence and has been given the security and the freedom of what we all hope for one day. We rejoice with her and bless God for remembering all of us and for 'doing great things for us' as he did once for Mary. And so today we are called to stand with Mary and Elizabeth and John and Jesus. We are called to let our souls proclaim the greatness of the Lord and let our spirits rejoice in God our Saviour. And who knows, perhaps one day we too will be called blessed because of our giving birth to the Word of God in our flesh and our world.

QUESTIONS

1. Mary greeted Elizabeth with the word 'shalom' – peace – and the Spirit stirred in Elizabeth causing her to cry out a blessing and words of truth that Mary needed to hear. Does your voice and your greeting of peace cause the Spirit to stir in others? Is there anyone in your life that is like Mary, whose greeting of peace and presence stirs your own soul to praise God?

2. Mary's response to Elizabeth's presence and words is to sing the wonders of God. Is there anyone in your life that just being in the presence of draws you to sing of God's goodness? And are you an Elizabeth for others, causing them to burst forth with joy and gratitude to God?

3. Mary dwells with the Trinity now. What can you do in your life so that you can live every day with the fullness of life that came to us through Mary's child? Ask Mary to draw you more deeply into God's presence now.

Twentieth Sunday in Ordinary Time

READINGS
PROV 9:1-6; PS 34; EPH 5:15-20; JN 6:51-58

> Watch how you live. Your lives may be the only Gospel your sisters
> and brothers will ever read.
>
> DOM HÉLDER CÂMARA

> I point out to you the stars, and all you saw was the tip of my finger.
>
> ARABIC PROVERB

The readings today take us back to Wisdom (as described in the book
of Proverbs) and to what we have been seeking to understand in our
own lives and relationships. Our life with God is Wisdom. Wisdom is
a gift found in words, stories, poetry, song and psalms. How we express
this in our heart of hearts, and how we share this with others is the
Body of Christ in the world. It is us, as Church and as Eucharist. We
are to be the wise ones of the world, for we feast on wisdom daily in
her food of the Scriptures and the wine that she has mixed. We are to
advance in the way of understanding, in the ways of God.

Jesus says over and over that anyone who eats his flesh and drinks
his blood shares in his sacrifice and remains in him as he remains
in them. The word 'remains' also means abides and dwells, as when
applied to a home, a sanctuary, a refuge or a place of peace. In Zen,
one is exhorted to 'take refuge in the Buddha, the dharma and the
sangha', that is, in Buddha, the community and the teachings. In our
tradition, we take refuge and abide in Jesus – the Body of Christ that
is both community and Eucharist. And once we are drawn into the
Trinity at Baptism, we are fed on Jesus' presence in the community
and the bread and wine that we share. Our liturgy is the place where
we are invited ever more deeply into the wisdom of God's own life,
knowledge and ways of loving.

When we gather to study the Word of God and seek to incorporate
it, to embody it in our own personal lives and in our communities,

we are entering Wisdom's house and sitting at her table. By eating together at this feast of the Word we really begin to live! When we gather to feast at the table of the Lord, and break bread sharing it with others and drink of the cup of wine then we are drawn together in communion with the Father, the Son and the Spirit – we dwell in the Trinity. God is at home in us and we are at home in God – always and everywhere – and it must begin to be seen by others that our lives are saturated with goodness and that we listen, obey and put into practice what we are learning to understand, that we are in awe before and with our God. This is real – real food and real drink – and this makes our life real, suffused with meaning and with grace.

Wisdom is the feminine manifestation or epiphany of God, and in this image she is the hostess who mixes the drinks, cooks the food and serves it, setting the table and inviting us into her house. Our gatherings are to be wise ones, with all equal at the table of Lady Wisdom, careful of one another and careful to be in communion: real unity born of struggle and dialogue, sourced in the Word of the Lord shared among us where we are all held accountable for our decisions, our relationships and our actions. We must really be living our resurrection life now, and if we feast on God then others must know and experience that in our presence.

These readings may begin to get to be too much for us. And again, we must remember that we are playing with and being held by Mystery, layered with many secret and hidden chambers. Now all that we can say about Jesus as flesh for the life of the world, the Bread of Life, the Word made flesh, and the Eucharist can also be said of Wisdom. Sometimes it is easier to speak in poetry or to sing of mystery and wisdom among us. For example, Brian Wren wrote the following hymn, 'I come with joy', which is often set to an American folk melody. Here are a few of the verses:

> I come with joy, a child of God,
> forgiven, loved and free,
> the life of Jesus to recall
> his love laid down for me.

I come with Christians far and near
to find, as all are fed,
the new community of love
in Christ's communion bread.

As Christ breaks bread and bids us share,
each proud division ends.
That love that made us, makes us one,
and strangers now are friends.

QUESTIONS

1. Share with a few others your favourite hymns and songs about the Eucharist. What new insights do they give you? How can these insights be translated into your daily life?

2. Wisdom is a gift we each received at Confirmation. It is the first gift to be able to see all of reality from God's point of view. Watch the news with others and talk about how you think God sees and responds to what is happening in your own country, in places where there is starvation, famine, violence, unrest and foolishness on the part of people in leadership positions who claim to be followers of Jesus. Do this on a regular basis so that fresh insights and the point of view of others in the Body of Christ can inform your understanding of the world.

3. So much of the imagery of this chapter in John weaves together food, eating, our bodies, the Body of Christ, broken and given for us and to us. It speaks of wisdom, the source of meaning and hope. Have a simple breaking of bread, some wine, and break open a piece of this chapter of John together with some friends. What do each of them make of this intricate mystery, this amazing gift and this shocking reality: that God is our food and we are to become that food for others?

Twenty-first Sunday in Ordinary Time

READINGS
JO 24:1-2, 15-17, 18; PS 34; EPH 5:21-32; JN 6:60-69

> Flesh feeds on the body and blood of Christ, that the soul may grow
> fat on God.
>
> TERTULLIAN

> Loving God, place a burden on our hearts today for your children
> across the world who are hungry. The thought of one billion
> chronically malnourished people on this earth is nearly inconceivable
> to us. But you, Lord, know each of these people by name. Give us
> the strength to act boldly to fight the sources of hunger around the
> world and in the United States. Amen.
>
> SOJOURNERS MAGAZINE

All three of this week's readings from John 6 ask challenging questions
of us: will we believe? Will we change? Will we commit ourselves to a
new belief and obedience to God? Joshua gathers the people together
with the elders, leaders, judges and officers. It is important that the
greatest among them be seen to commit themselves in public so that
they can be held accountable for their choices and words. Joshua
models those who will be ready to move forward into the promised
land with the words: 'As for me and my household, we will serve the
Lord.' Joshua and his people declare who they belong to and who they
will serve. The people first tell of the great deeds God has done for them
and then they declare together ritually: 'We also will serve the Lord,
for he is our God.' And so, today is a day for committing ourselves, not
just as individuals, but as families and parishes, to the service of the
Lord, for bringing others into his kingdom by sharing with them the
mysteries and the responsibilities of believing in Jesus, the Lord of life.

After the long discourse of Jesus with the crowd, the leadership
of the people and many of his followers realise it is now 'crunch' time.
Many are loud and vocal about how they feel about Jesus' teaching:
'This saying is hard; who can accept it?' Jesus is aware that what he

has been saying is shocking, even disturbing. He pushes them with the image of the Son of Man – a figure of judgement from the book of Daniel, who comes in glory although he has been tortured and has suffered. He comes to demand an account of all nations. He declares that his words are Spirit and life. And again, he refers to his Father who has sent him; his words are rooted in God the Father and the Spirit who sourced the universe at the very beginning (Genesis 1). Many of the disciples decide they cannot take it and we are told that they returned to their former way of life and no longer accompanied him. We are faced with this same choice today.

Jesus has declared: 'I am the living bread for the life of the world. Anyone who eats my flesh and drinks my blood has eternal life, dwells in me and I in them and they will be raised up.' What do we think about this shocking statement? Does it even shock us? It's supposed to! In our present translations the word used for 'eat my flesh' is hard enough to take, but the origin words for 'to eat' were ones that had the sense of chewing and then eating like an animal that was ravenously hungry: 'gnawing at the flesh and pulling it apart', as a wild animal would take the flesh off the carcass it had just taken down. Many of us would resist this image – we have made Eucharist a ritual that is distanced from eating, or anything that deals with the flesh of Jesus. And yet I was once startled to see in an old Irish translation of the Prologue of John's Gospel the line 'and the Word became flesh and dwells among us' translated 'and the Word became meat and dwells among us'. These words of Jesus about his person, Word, his life, his gift of staying with us as food in the Eucharist is much stronger and demanding than we are often wont to think of it.

This food – the Bread of Life, the Word of the Lord, the presence of the Crucified and Risen Lord among us – is food for the way, the way of the cross, the way of God's power and reign of justice and peace in the world. God demands that we live with integrity, with love for one another, even unto death, if we are to call ourselves followers of Jesus, the Son of Man and the Bread of Life. Jesus confronted them with the truth and he does so again today with us: 'I know that some of you do not believe.' Can Jesus look at us singularly and as a community and say those words and know that they are true still? Perhaps the only difference is that we continue with our old way of life and don't really accompany Jesus on the way. We just visit on occasion or say we believe without actions, decisions and a way of life that reveals our obedience to and service of the Lord of life. This is easier to do today, because we can continue to go to church on Sundays and do devotional practices and yet, as individuals and often as the bulk of a parish, we have to be aware of being communities of the Body of Christ, ensuring we are not simply people who go to the same building on Sunday.

QUESTIONS

1. Today is a good time to renew our baptismal promises as a parish at all the liturgies. Listen to them in the context of obeying and serving Jesus as the Bread of Life. Do you promise to live in the freedom of the children of God? Do you promise to resist evil and refuse to be mastered by any sin, violence, evil or injustice? Do you promise to live under no sign of power but the sign of the cross, in the name of the Father, the Son and the Holy Spirit? (Remember, the baptismal promises are all in the plural.)

2. Paul's letter begins with the words: 'defer to one another out of reverence to Christ' (a better rendering of the verb than 'be subordinate'). Because of the Incarnation, we must now be as reverent and careful of all others as we would be with the person of Jesus, the Body of Christ in our midst. Sometimes that is hardest in our own families, in our most intimate relationships. Spend time today – as family and friends – and talk about your relationships as the Body of Christ in the larger Body of Christ the Church.

3. Jesus turns to us with the words: 'Do you want to leave me too?' Peter's response is hardly passionate or steeped in faith: 'Lord, to whom shall we go?' Today we need to ask for a surge in our faith, in our wisdom and understanding so that we will not betray Jesus as Peter did. A way to do this is to use the psalm refrain as a prayer over and over: 'Taste and see the goodness of the Lord'.

Twenty-second Sunday in Ordinary Time

READINGS

DEUT 4:1-2, 6-8; PS 15; JAS 1:17-18, 21-22, 27; MK 7:1-8, 14-15, 21-23

> Honour the tradition but expand the understanding. That's what religions must do right now if they hope to be helpful to humans in the years ahead.
>
> NEALE DONALD WALSCH

Once again we return to Mark's Gospel, from now until the last Sunday of the year, Christ the King. Changing Gospels can be disorienting and difficult. Mark's Gospel was the first, and John's the last in our tradition in the Lectionary. Both have drastically different styles, written for different communities probably as much as forty years apart. Perhaps the only thing they bear in common is that they were both written in times of terrific persecution, but even then, Mark's community was struggling with the Judeo-Roman war and its consequences, whereas John's community was trying to survive during a long wave of Roman persecution, both brutal and far-ranging across the empire.

We return now to Mark and to one of Jesus' many confrontations with the Jewish elders and teachers. They are intent on tripping him up, questioning him in such a way that he has to defend not only his own words and actions, but those of his disciples. It is much like being on trial all the time and the first time you trip up, the evidence is gathered against you. In some ways, the outcome is already decided upon: it just has to appear that you deserve the verdict. Those who attack Jesus are interested in traditions of custom, ritual, long-standing ways of doing things, and Jesus is interested in the core, the heart of religion, in what God is interested in as we express and practice our faith.

All the readings are about practice, about putting priorities into our way of living and of concentrating on the essence of the Good News. In that sense, the readings are like lessons to be learned, and tried out, experienced with others so that we learn to incorporate them into our routines and our public expression of daily living. The Pharisees and scribes are interested in details that they feel must be observed and there isn't much of a difference around which traditions might be more important than others. All bear the same weight and therefore the same punishment or dismissal if breached.

Jesus has no patience with this sort of religious piety – externals and details that are 'for show', to reveal that one knows all the particulars of tradition, but which are easier to perform than the core practice of what it means to obey the laws and honour the covenant with God. Jesus quotes Isaiah to them, calling them hypocrites: 'This people honours me with their lips, but their hearts are far from me. In vain do they worship me, teaching human precepts as dogma. You forsake the commandment of God and hold to human tradition.' Jesus deals with the leaders, teachers and preachers bluntly, and then turns to the crowd and goes straight for their hearts and the source of their actions. Perhaps the last evil and violent behaviour that he lists is the one that speaks the most truth: an obtuse spirit.

Moses exhorts the people to hear and obey the statutes that reveal wisdom and the presence of God among his people, so that the nations may be in awe and be drawn to the worship of this God. And the letter of James drives home Jesus' insistence on actually embodying one's belief in actions and in practices that reveal the compassion, the justice and the truth of God. Religion that is pure and undefiled before God and the Father is this: to care for orphans and widows in their affliction and to keep oneself unstained by the world. It is important to remember that when the word 'world' is used in the Scriptures, it primarily means the dominant political, nationalistic, economic and social structures that demand obedience to their rules and regulations to the detriment of what is right and just.

James puts forth a simple and direct command: 'Humbly welcome the word that has been planted in you and be doers of the word and not hearers only.' We start over in these months to live the resurrection life begun in our Baptism and to live with more integrity, more passion and more care. We concentrate less on details and traditions and more on the heart of our religion. Today we are faced with Jesus' contempt for those who are more concerned with their own enforcement of side issues, ways to pray and worship, to eat, to perform devotions and even practice bodily habits, rather than obey God's demands that we be Good News to the Poor, and love one another as God has loved us in Jesus. We need to ask ourselves if Jesus would find good cause to call us heretics and to turn away from us to speak the truth to those who will listen. As uncomfortable as that makes us feel, we must look at our traditions and accretions, to examine whether or not they have anything to do with taking care of the least of our brothers and sisters and honouring God in them?

QUESTIONS

1. The lessons today are, in a sense, about what constitutes 'true religion'. All too often we can get bogged down in right ritual, or in thinking 'that's the way we've always done it' or 'but so-and-so says this is the way you're supposed to do it'. It is much easier to take sides, argue and do nothing except ignore the reality of those in need and what God really wants of us – to practice his compassion and graciousness to those most in jeopardy. What are some traditions and details that keep you and your parish from actually doing the corporal works of mercy or from making sure that everyone in your neighbourhood gets to church or is visited and cared for?

2. What human regulations or 'dogmas', using Jesus' term, get in the way of our being the Body of Christ, so that others around us can see that we are obedient to God's covenant to us in the Crucified and Risen Lord?

3. Worship and justice are two sides of one hand, though we more often than not concentrate on one more than the other. In your parish, which side of the hand is ignored, or just given lip-service? How can you, in small groups, get to the core of what needs to be done as the Body of Christ in your neighbourhood and city or country?

Twenty-third Sunday in Ordinary Time

READINGS

IS 35:4-7; PS 146; JAS 2:1-5; MK 7:31-37

> In the stillness of the quiet, if we listen, we can hear the whisper of the
> heart giving strength to weakness, courage to fear, hope to despair.
>
> HOWARD THURMAN

> Always give good heed to the Word of God, whether you hear or read
> it in private, or hearken to it when publicly preached. Listen with
> attention and reverence, seek to profit by it, and do not let precious
> words fall unheeded but receive them into your heart.
>
> FRANCIS DE SALES

The reading from Isaiah is gloriously hopeful and filled with courage
– a reading for Advent, our God coming towards us with movement,
energy and power, like the streams bursting forth in the desert and
cascading down the steppe, with even the burning sands turning into
cool pools, water everywhere. The result is that our God is tangible.
The eyes of the blind are opened, the ears of the deaf cleared and even
the lame begin to leap and dance for joy and the tongues of the mute
will sing. There are swings from one extreme to the other, all in the
direction of life ever more abundantly for those who were lacking so
much. So much of Isaiah's joy and the story of Jesus with a deaf man is
connected and bound up to each of us in our Baptism. It is important
to note that this story takes place outside of Israel in pagan territory
among those who are not Jews but have heard of Jesus.

Listen to the prayer from the baptismal rite called the 'Ephphatha',
the same word Jesus groans out as he puts his fingers in the man's ears
and spits on his tongue: 'The Lord Jesus made the deaf hear and the
dumb speak. May he touch your ears to receive his Word, and your
mouth to proclaim his faith, to the praise and glory of God the Father.'

Our initiation into the Body of Christ opens our senses, our minds
and our hearts to be able to hear God as Jesus hears God, and so to
listen to and obey. Much of what is found in the Word of the Lord, in

the Gospels, Acts and letters such as that of James, is hard to accept. Yet to hear is to believe and to listen is to obey. Our Baptism is our beginnings and we spend the rest of our lives learning how to listen and take the Word of God to heart within us so that it transforms every area of our lives.

Surprisingly, when the man's ears are unblocked, his speech impediment, his inability to form words that could be understood, is removed! He speaks plainly. He is given voice to speak of what God is doing now in the world. The implied unblocking of our ears also opens a lifeline to our hearts and voices, so that we can speak words that need to be heard by others, and taken to heart. Often that entails asking hard questions and pointing out the blindness and deafness of those around us. James tells us that we are blind and deaf to the poor and yet we listen to every word that the rich have to say, making sure that they sit close to us. James uses the word 'listen' often. And when he does, like Jesus, our eyes and our ears are being brought into balance so that we can see how our faith is being put into practice or denied by our actions and behaviour. The Word of the Lord seeks to open our eyes and unblock our ears and hearts so that we can see the way God sees and treat others with justice and integrity.

Jesus orders the friends of the deaf mute not to tell anyone, but of course they do! In fact, they spread it around, telling the story to anyone who will listen. Why does Jesus so often tell people not to say something about him and what he has done for them? This is an important question. Most people whom Jesus healed, even his own disciples, have their own idea of who he is and what he's doing. Jesus doesn't want them saying what they think about him, but rather to hear what he says about himself and the Father. In a sense, the deaf mute is all of Jesus' disciples who can't hear what he is saying and speak only their own narrow desires rather than the Truth about who Jesus is and what he is trying to do among us. And of course, we too are deaf-mutes often saying what we want others to hear rather than speaking plainly about who Jesus is and what he says about himself in the Gospel. This is the theme of this week's Gospel readings.

Our ears have been opened, our lips unsealed, our tongues loosened and first of all we are to be bearers of joy, of hope, of freedom and the glory of God among us – as Isaiah sings. We are to make sure that what Jesus has done for us, we in turn do for others. It was others that brought the deaf-mute to Jesus, now we must be those who bring others to Jesus so that their lives might be opened and stretched and that they too might find their voice to bless God.

QUESTIONS

1. James speaks to the issue of favouritism in his community, specifically between the rich and the poor, but favouritism is usually based on the biases of the dominant culture and groups: the educated over the ignorant, position over powerlessness, one race over another, those with religious power over those who are 'just believers'. How does favouritism present itself in your parish? And what would Jesus be saying to you and your parish in this situation? Who do you think he'd be sitting with and making sure to speak with afterwards?

2. God in history, through the prophets, and especially in Jesus, restores, heals, opens, stretches, reforms, changes, makes new, fills up what is lacking, reverses positions. Is the way we see things and the way we hear people somehow the reverse of God's perspective? Who do you tend not to listen to or even notice in church? Have a short conversation with someone you never speak to at church and see what you can hear and what God might be saying to you.

Twenty-fourth Sunday in Ordinary Time

READINGS
IS 50:4-9A; PS 116; JAS 2:14-18; MK 8:27-35

> The matter is quite simple. The Bible is very easy to understand. But we as Christians are a bunch of scheming swindlers. We pretend to be unable to understand it because we know very well that the minute we understand we are obliged to act accordingly. Take any words in the New Testament and forget everything except pledging yourself to act accordingly. My God, you will say, if I do that my whole life will be ruined.
>
> SØREN KIERKEGAARD

The readings for the next few Sundays make us feel like we are in Lent – facing who Jesus is, the depth of his demands and whether or not we are living like followers of Jesus. More so, they insist that we look at who we think Jesus is and what following him will mean if we are truthful and align ourselves with his priorities. Who is Jesus? In answer, we are provided with three powerful readings from Isaiah, James and Mark. And often, there is a gulf between our perception of Jesus, that of the Scripture writers and Jesus' own words. This gulf is apparent not only in our words, but in our prayers, our expressions of faith and most strongly in our practice, or lack of practice, as disciples. In Isaiah, Jesus is an 'open ear that hears God and does not rebel or turn back', even when he is assailed, persecuted, tortured and publicly humiliated. Jesus is faithful, 'setting his face like flint', steeling himself against those that oppose him, with God as his help upholding him. This is the Jesus who speaks truth to power, who sides with those who are the victims of violence and injustice and who confronts people with the contradictions of their words and religious practices, their brutality and inhumanity towards their brothers and sisters in the world.

The reading from Mark is a turning point in his Gospel and denotes the second major call to conversion: the first is the calling to be a disciple in the tradition of the prophets in the company of Jesus and to catch men and women in the net of the kingdom of God's power and rule in the world. This challenge is the call to face the reality of rejection, persecution – even torture, crucifixion and death – because of obedience to Jesus' words. The questioning of the disciples by Jesus takes place at Caesarea Philippi, small villages built in the shadow of the empire of Rome, whose rule had forced the inhabitants to live as slaves in their own country, occupied by the Roman army and pillaged. Jesus demands to know if they, and if we, follow the empire's values and idols, or if we are committed to following his preaching and his embodiment of God as justice and compassion, peace and forgiveness. Crucifixion was the usual form of capital punishment for anyone who was not a Roman citizen, reserved for those who were a threat to the power and domination of Rome. And this is Jesus' end.

'Who do people say that I am?' The answer is sure: John the Baptist, Elijah, one of the prophets. The people know, more than the disciples, the tradition of Jesus. The prophets were the 'troublers' of Israel and they suffered for the truth of their words. Jesus then questions them: who do you say that I am? Peter answers: 'the Christ'. He's sure he has the right answer, but Jesus warns them not to say that about him to anyone, because he is not! The Messiah for the majority of people, including the disciples, is a nationalistic leader who will drive the Romans out of their land, restore the temple and the kingdom of Israel and make them a force in the world again. This is so far from who Jesus is that to call him the Messiah can only be confusing. And so he begins to tell them about who he is – the Son of Man – and that his future is one of rejection, crucifixion and resurrection. This is not what any of them want to hear and Peter reacts and contradicts Jesus, he rebukes him and, in essence, begins to renounce and deny Jesus in this moment.

And Jesus issues his call to us to come after him, to deny ourselves, so that we will not deny him, take up our cross and follow him. He realistically tells us that we have to be willing to lose everything we value, even our lives, so that we can actually have and live his own life and make the Gospel a reality. In losing the ways of the empire and power of nations, we are saving our integrity and our souls. The cross is offered to us to bear our share of the burden of the Gospel, to fill up what is lacking in the sufferings of Christ, to commit ourselves to solidarity with all victims and so to walk the way with Jesus to the cross and glory.

QUESTIONS

1. Peter balks at Jesus' words and rebukes him, telling Jesus what he's supposed to do – the Gospel according to Peter. Do you find yourself telling Jesus what he's supposed to do for you and how your life is supposed to be? Jesus reacts to Peter's resistance and refusal to look at the truth with some of the strongest words in the Gospel. What's it like to hear Jesus' words: 'Get behind me, Satan. You're not thinking like God does; you're thinking the way people do who have not heard my words!' Remember that the word 'Satan' means hinderer; are we hindering Jesus' word from being heard in the world? Are we hindering Jesus from doing what needs to be done for others: the poor, victims of injustice and violence because this is not what we want?

2. 'Who do you say that I am?' When Jesus poses that question to you, what will you answer?

Twenty-fifth Sunday in Ordinary Time

READINGS
WIS 2:12, 17-20; PS 54; JAS 3:16–4:3; MK 9:30-37

> We've got to get this thing right. What is needed is a realisation that power without love is reckless and abusive, and love without power is sentimental and anaemic. Power at its best is love implementing the demands of justice, and justice at its best is power correcting everything that stands against love. It is precisely this collision of immoral power with powerless morality which constitutes the major crisis of our time.
>
> MARTIN LUTHER KING, JR

> Imagine yourself to be the servant of all, and look upon all as if they were Christ our Lord in person. And thus shall you do him honour and reverence.
>
> TERESA OF AVILA

This Gospel is a private discussion with Jesus as they travel and he teaches. It is a lesson in wisdom, not in the ways of the dominating culture, but in the ways of God in Jesus, the Son of Man 'who will be handed over to other men and they will kill him, but he will rise.' The reaction of the disciples to these words of Jesus are confusion and fear. They have just been commanded to follow him and pick up their cross and now Jesus is being more specific in the treachery to come, and the suffering and death that is before him. This title, the Son of Man, is the one that Jesus uses repeatedly to describe himself, and his role in living, dying, rising, judging and coming in glory. He is the just one, the Beloved Son, the child of God who is cared for and cherished by God, but who is not saved from suffering, and from being human, and so dying. This image first appears in the Book of Daniel in one of the visions. There is one like a 'Son of Man' who comes in glory on the clouds of heaven, his face and garments radiant. He comes to judge the nations with justice and he himself has suffered unjustly at the hands of all. It is a mixture of the titles of the Lamb of God in Exodus, the

Suffering Servant of Isaiah Crucified and Risen One, and the Lamb in the Book of Revelation. The reading from Wisdom also describes some of who he is: 'Let us see whether his words be true; let us find out what will happen to him. For if the just one be the son of God, he will defend him and deliver him from the hand of his foes' (Wis 2:17-18).

But the disciples won't engage with the depth of what they are being told. Instead they get petty and pretentious about which one of them is the greatest! When Jesus asked them what they were talking about, they should have been utterly ashamed and exposed for their selfishness, arrogance, petty jealousies and ambition. This is what the letter of James describes: what we are not supposed to be if we are following Jesus, the child of God. And so Jesus speaks to them patiently, telling them that they are to be the last, the least, the servant of all, if they want to be first in his family and following. Then he takes a child – randomly from the street – and sits in the middle of the disciples, the Twelve, and wraps his arms around the child with intimacy and vulnerability, and tells them: 'Whoever receives one child in my name, receives me; and whoever receives me, receives the One who sent me'. An enormous amount of theology is being shared in this gesture and in these words.

First they are referred to as the Twelve, which means he is speaking to them in the capacity of being leaders, models and those who exercise power – and it must be Jesus' power, not their own versions. At the time of Jesus, children had no power at all. They were devalued and expendable, useful, but not a priority. In those terms they were equivalent to slaves, outcasts, the poor and socially rejected. They had to obey anyone older than they were.

This image went against everything in culture, society and religion. The power of the child was a power that was meek, without violence, humble, patient, peaceful, merciful, sincere, faithful and righteous (meaning holy and just). A child is the symbol of those Jesus aligns himself with – those without strength, dominance, access to structures or a place in society. These are all the characteristics in the letter of James, written to the Beloved in his community. This is the wisdom of God. This is the power of the Son of Man.

Jesus' power lies in the Father, who protects him, stands behind him, supports him, defends him – especially when he is handed over to the ridicule and harsh treatment of others, mocked and vilified because of his words of truth, misunderstood and rejected by his own followers and friends and brutally murdered. Jesus' wisdom teaching is demanding and upsetting. It is in conflict with society's values and most people's personal ambitions and hopes. They are told that Jesus does not tolerate any use of power that is competitive, self-serving, harsh, proud or aggrandising. And the Twelve are told that they are to welcome 'a child' – that is, all the poor and those without position, prestige or power – as he does, embracing them and drawing them in with the hospitality of God. To welcome, care for and align oneself with 'a child' is to align oneself with Jesus and with the One who sent Jesus. To reject any 'child' is to reject Jesus and the Father. Once again, we are being asked to come after Jesus in his own manner and style, rather than to spend our time with each other discussing who's the greatest, the first among us and refusing to talk about the words of Jesus that we find difficult.

QUESTIONS

1. Jesus tells the Twelve that the way we treat others is the way we are treating Jesus and the One who sent him among us. What are we saying to God with our actions or lack of welcoming to others?

2. What do you think Jesus would have to say about how we, as individuals and as Church, 'receive the children of the earth' today: immigrants, street people, those just out of rehab and prison, those society shuns?

3. Jesus keeps telling us that he is the Son of Man. Try praying to the Son of Man come to judge the nations with justice.

Twenty-sixth Sunday in Ordinary Time

READINGS

NUM 11:25-29; PS 19; JAS 5:1-6; MK 9:38-43, 45, 47-48

> If God's incomprehensibility does not grip us in a word, if it does
> not draw us into our super-luminous darkness, if it does not call us
> out of the little house of our homely, close-hugged truths ... we have
> misunderstood the words of Christianity.
>
> KARL RAHNER

> The more we let each voice sing out with its own true tone, the richer
> will be the diversity of the chant in unison.
>
> ANGELUS SILESIUS

Last week we heard Jesus telling and then showing his disciples, as
leaders in his community, to be welcoming and inclusive, and to
draw into the heart of the circle of God's embrace all those who are
on the fringes of society, and all those who are considered without
stature or power in the world. Now we have readings about leaders
who aren't only unwelcoming to outsiders, but are judgemental about
who might be considered 'one of us' and about who should be allowed
proximity to Jesus. The disciples are resistant to what Jesus is trying
to share about his family and his kingdom and about how they are to
act towards others.

The Gospel begins with John, Jesus' younger cousin, reporting and
complaining that someone who isn't one of them was doing something
good in the name of Jesus and that they tried to stop him! This is the
insider's club par excellence, deciding who's worthy to be in and who's
out and what people should do in the name of Jesus. Jesus has an
incredible depth of patience. He tells them that 'no one can perform
a mighty deed in my name who can at the same time speak ill of me'.
First of all, the leaders of Jesus' community must realise and remember
that God works in all peoples, religions, situations, circumstances, and
that you don't have to be a member of the Church, or a parish, or a

religious community, or affiliated with any group in the Church to be acting in the name of Jesus and doing mighty deeds that are sourced in Jesus! God's range and the reign of God is far wider and more inclusive than that of the Church or the span and influence of its leaders.

We are never to belittle others who do good. Anyone who does justice, does good, welcomes another – who isn't 'one of us' yet treats us the way Jesus would – will not only be rewarded but they are to be considered 'with us.' It seems that the Twelve's obsession with who has the power and last word within their group also bleeds out into deciding who is worthy of doing great things for God, with Jesus. One wonders if paying so much attention to what others are doing, and denigrating their actions, is a good excuse not to look at themselves. And so the Gospel continues with some very harsh words. We must look to our own behaviour and the effects it has on others, especially on those who are weak. Jesus uses hyperbole to try to hammer home the effect our actions and words can have on each other – their long-ranging and destructive consequences which we are mostly unaware of and ignore. The more power and position one has in the kingdom of Jesus, the more one is held accountable for our behaviour and attitudes and how they impact on others. We are to look to the works of our hands, where we go, how we travel, what we see and do not see. We are to examine our daily lives in detail to make sure that we are not making it difficult for others already hard-pressed by life.

The letter of James details some of the practices that have repercussions on others' lives. These include withholding wages and treating those who harvest the food miserly so that they do not even eat of their labours. They are things that are embedded in our culture and society and that we may therefore find difficult to break away from. It could be the accumulation of wealth that we hoard and do not use for the benefit of others. It may be to live in luxury and pleasure without concern for others or to participate and be in collusion with violence that destroys others. All these are horrors to God, though often Christians live this way, and as long as they are practicing religion, they believe themselves to be 'in' and saved. Today Jesus looks at us and warns us: don't be so sure you're not the ones that are hindering my ways on earth and that should be judged; don't be quick to accuse others of a misdeed who aren't 'your kind' when in reality they are 'with us'.

QUESTIONS

1. In the reading about Moses, almost the same thing is happening as with the Twelve. Moses has asked God for others to lead with him, to be made prophets. God obliges by sending the Spirit upon seventy of the elders, even on two who weren't gathered with the rest of them but were still in their own tents. And it is Joshua, who will lead in Moses' place one day, who exhorts Moses to stop the men from speaking in the Spirit. Who do you know that speaks the Spirit of God today in our Church and outside the Church who is often told that they don't have that power, or shouldn't be doing so?

2. Moses prays: 'Would that all the people of the Lord were prophets! Would that the Lord might bestow his spirit on them all!' We believe that this has happened in Baptism and Confirmation – the Spirit is given to all the people of God, the Body of Christ. God speaks in many people: how do you recognise someone speaking the truth of Jesus?

Twenty-seventh Sunday in Ordinary Time

READINGS

GEN 2:18-24; PS 128; HEB 2:9-11; MK 10:2-16

> By the love of man and woman a thread is wound that stretches to
> the heart of the world.
>
> PIERRE TEILHARD DE CHARDIN

> To be is to stand for and what human beings stand for is the great
> mystery of being God's partner.
>
> RABBI ABRAHAM JOSHUA HESCHEL

For the next few Sundays the readings will look at the basics of our
practice which reveal what we believe about God, our relationships
and how to live in the world. In some ways, it will be a broad-based
examination of conscience and a chance to review where we are in
our following of Jesus. We are moving quickly towards the end of
the Church year, and so some reflective questioning and reminders
may be exactly what we all, as Church, need at this time. We begin by
looking at relationships. The primary one for many human beings is
institutionalised by society as marriage and is a sacrament for believers.
But all relationships for those baptised into the Body of Christ are
rooted in God first. We go back to our beginnings in Genesis, to a
creation story that is devised to look at the making of human beings,
as male and female in the image of God, but that is also a story about
family, generations and marriage.

It begins with the essence of being human: that it is not good
for man to be alone. As man names all the creatures that God has
created, he does not find one that is like him who can be his partner,
his companion, his equal in revealing God. And so God creates woman,
another human being, a counter-balance, drawn from the ribs that
protect the lungs and heart. And God brings her to the man. She is
not named (Adam is not the man's name, but a description of what
he is made from, literally meaning a groundling or earthling). The

primary relationship is not father or mother to child but adult human to adult human.

In the Gospel reading from Mark, the Pharisees set Jesus up so that however he answers their questions he will set one faction off as having the right answer, inferring that the other faction is obviously wrong. The first issue is that of a man divorcing his wife (a wife was unable to divorce her husband). The Pharisees already know the answer enshrined in the law and Jesus makes them acknowledge this. He then takes them by surprise and says that this particular piece of the law only exists because of the 'hardness of your hearts'. The Pharisees are obsessed with the letter of law and with the reasons or conditions for divorce according to existing practice. Jesus however is concerned with faithfulness in marriage, by both parties. As demonstrated in the creation story, marriage is about faithfulness and clinging to one another for companionship, in service and obedience to God and as a way of being human together on earth.

Jesus will not validate the Pharisees' position on divorce. Later the disciples question him – they are having trouble with Jesus' response. Jesus tries to tell them that both man and woman are to be faithful in a marriage – the relationship involves man, woman and God. The law is for all equally, all equally stubborn and hard of heart. Jesus does not condemn either but is clear that both are called to honour that commitment.

Then what follows seems disconnected but is, in fact, an answer to looking at relationships through the lens of law, rather than love. People are bringing their children to Jesus and the disciples are trying to stop them. Jesus is indignant and rebukes them: 'Let the children come to me; do not hinder them, for the kingdom of God belongs to such as these … whoever does not accept the kingdom of God like a child will not enter it.' In essence, we must stop acting like the Pharisees and the disciples. We must stop making the law serve us, or certain groups, and make sure that it is for all. We must become like the children of God who serve those who are outcast, poor and considered unworthy to approach Jesus and not hinder them because they have no power or because we feel they have no right. We must become lowly, obedient and powerless or else we will not enter God's rule. Like the Pharisees and the disciples we have a lot to learn. We have a long way to go in growing up to be adult children of God, intent on being faithful, as Jesus is, in marriage, in family, in all our relationships and in Church and the world.

QUESTIONS

1. Perhaps there are some basic principles to remember when it comes to marriage and family. The couple concentrates on their relationship to each other while each one works on their relationship to God. Then together, they work on their relationship to God in the Trinity that was witness to their marriage. Lastly the couple needs others in community, those who are single and married, to share the Scriptures, to hold each other accountable for growth and change, for support and friendship. A couple cannot make it on their own – no one can. Who are some of the couples in your community who are the friends of God, good friends for each other, and for others?

2. Christian marriage is supposed to be very different than civil marriage, which is concerned with sexuality, procreation, the inheritance system and the structuring of society. For Catholics, marriage is an image of the Trinity, the three of them together, open to drawing others into their life and love – children, and others who share their belief and hopes. Who are your other friends of God that are essential to your marriage and your children's lives?

Twenty-eighth Sunday in Ordinary Time

READINGS

WIS 7:7-11; PS 90; HEB 4:12-13; MK 10:17-30

> As long as there is poverty in the world I can never be rich, even if I
> have a billion dollars. As long as diseases are rampant and millions
> of people in this world cannot expect to live more than twenty-eight
> to thirty years, I can never be totally healthy even if I just got a good
> check-up at Mayo Clinic. I can never be what I ought to be until
> you are what you ought to be. This is the way our world is made. No
> individual or nation can stand out boasting of being independent.
> We are interdependent.
>
> MARTIN LUTHER KING, JR

> I find ecstasy in living. The mere sense of living is joy enough.
>
> EMILY DICKINSON

These Sundays we are looking at the big-ticket issues – today it is money, power, influence, sharing, the poor, and how hard it is to get into God's kingdom if we are wealthy. The way of many societies is contrasted with the way of God. We begin with a reading from Wisdom: the writer prayed and prudence was given, then he pleaded and wisdom was given. Do we pray for these values and gifts of insight? Do we really want to see the way God sees? To apportion out our riches, possessions, time, intensity, work and energies on God's priorities and to know what is enough?

The reading from Hebrews reminds us that the Word we are proclaiming today and all days is sharper than any two-edged sword, going straight for our guts, hearts and minds, deep into our joints and marrow! A double-edged sword is razor sharp on one side and jagged on the other – it slices through skin, organs and bones and then rips again coming out. We are giving a shocking image that is appropriate today, for Jesus' words do shock us. The story is about a man called to follow Jesus more closely. He kneels before Jesus and asks the question: 'What must I do to inherit eternal life?' Jesus reminds him of the commandments and the man's response is shocking: he's observed all of them since he was young!

And so Jesus takes a risk: we are told that he looks at the man, loves him and tells him: 'you are lacking in one thing.' Rarely do we hear of Jesus looking at someone and loving them. He does, of course, but the fact that it is stated here says something about this man in particular. Jesus tells him what he's lacking and it is not what he wanted to hear or what we want to hear either: 'Go, sell what you have, and give to the poor and you will have treasure in heaven; then come, follow me.' The treasure of the kingdom lies in touching and knowing the poor and sharing with them. He is not being told to beggar himself, but to sell his excess and then share it with others who need it. Jesus is inviting him into his inner circle, to a level of relationship with him that is intimate and close.

Of course, today Jesus is looking at each of us with love and is ready to tell us the one thing we are lacking! And it is the same for all of us. We can believe in Jesus, obey the laws, but if we want to know Jesus more intimately, than we must shed our extra skins and what we collect that we rely on, and care more about than we do the poor and God's priorities of justice, peace and abundant life for all.

The man goes away sad because of all he clings to – all that possesses him. Jesus continues to shock with his words: 'Children, how hard it is to enter the kingdom of God!' and he uses the outrageous image of a camel going through the eye of a needle: if you're rich that's how slim your chances are for entering God's home. The entrance lies through the poor, in generosity and paring down to what you need. We pray this daily in the Our Father – 'give us today our daily bread', just enough for today for everyone – but in reality do we want our prayer answered?

Jesus' disciples are shocked. Who's going to get in? It was a common belief, and still is in many Christian circles, that riches are a blessing from God. In reality, the tradition was that most wealth was gained by exploitation, injustice and selfishness. Jesus explains that nothing is impossible with God – even the rich can let go of what they've stored up and share with others, even that is not impossible with grace! Stretching the truth by a long way, Peter immediately declares that they've given up everything to follow Jesus. Jesus assures them: whatever you give up, you will get a hundred-fold back here and now! How? We will know these blessings in community, in faith, and life shared with others – new brothers, sisters, mothers, children, lands, houses everywhere in the world. But it comes along with persecution too, just to live with such open-handedness and open-heartedness makes people edgy and reveals how much of our lives reek with self-righteousness. We perform the basic observances, but do we do any more than that? What does Jesus feel when we are given the truth and we prefer our security, our acquisitions and the place we've worked so hard for, to his risky and wild invitation to come and follow?

QUESTIONS

1. Sometimes this story is called 'The Thirteenth Disciple'. It makes us nervous because each time we truly meet Jesus we are being looked at with love and asked for a deeper relationship that entails change on our part. Reflect on whether or not you act like the man in the story, or even like the disciples, thinking they've given up all for Jesus.

2. God is generous beyond our imaginings. Even when we give God so little or share so little with the poor among us, we are overwhelmed with that hundred-fold in return. What kinds of gifts have you been given, often in return for things that you really didn't need in the first place?

3. Each time we hear this Gospel, Jesus is going to look at us and say: 'there is one more thing that you are lacking'. God wants us all – heart, mind, soul, body – all we have and are. What do you think God would like you to share with the poor? What do you think Jesus is asking your parish, your diocesan Church, to share with others? Will Jesus go away sad yet again?

Twenty-ninth Sunday in Ordinary Time

READINGS
IS 53:10-11; PS 33; HEB 4:14-16; MK 10:35-45

> When Jesus bids us come and follow him, he bids us come and die.
> DIETRICH BONHOEFFER

> The greatness of a community is most accurately measured by the compassionate actions of its members, a heart of grace and a soul generated by love.
> CORETTA SCOTT KING

We continue looking at our lives and whether or not they reflect Jesus' way of being in the world. Today the readings deal with suffering, service and power. And again, Jesus' words are a shock to our system. We know what he is saying, but we just don't like it, and often we have no intention of putting it into practice in our lives. We begin with a reading from Isaiah, the suffering servant prophet, as he seeks to derive meaning from the suffering of the innocent. He says: 'Through his suffering, my servant shall justify many, and their guilt he shall bear'. There are so many whose lives reflect this reality. There are so many who suffer at the hands of others, as a result of poor economic, political decisions and actions. The words of Isaiah are, at best, cold comfort that 'they will see light in fullness of days and see their descendants in a long life'. Reality contradicts this often in life, but if we transfer these words to the person of Jesus they are foundational to our belief. We believe in the cross and the resurrection experienced here, and one day we believe in the fullness of light and life.

The Gospel story reveals humanity at its basest. James and John, Jesus' cousins, attempt to set Jesus up by the wording of their request: 'Teacher, we want you to do for us whatever we ask of you.' And what they want is power, authority, prestige, position and glory by association – seats at Jesus' left and right. Previous to this, Jesus has been telling them that the Son of Man will be rejected, handed over to be tortured, crucified and murdered. They don't want to hear about it, they have their own plans and their own reasons for being with and staying with Jesus. What must Jesus have thought and felt about this reaction from those who are supposedly his friends and followers?

Jesus tries to tell them that they don't have a clue what they're asking for – he has told them about the cross, but they are ignoring those statements. He asks them if they can drink the cup and endure the Baptism that he will drink, and they blithely say 'we can'. But what they ask for is not Jesus' to give. It will be given to criminals – terrorists that moved against Roman power and paid the price, along with Jesus whose very person threatened all authority and power based on violence, fear and insecurity. The other disciples get wind of what James and John have been up to and are furious. They are busy jealously fighting over their own position, still refusing to listen to Jesus' words or warning, his invitation to follow him to the cross and to share in his power.

Jesus' religion – his devotion to his Father in the power of the Spirit – is unlike any religion in the world. And those who would have power in his community must not legitimise their own authority, or use their authority to validate their decisions, to enforce their acceptance or to lord it over anyone. Instead they are to be known by their service, their attitude to being a slave who is at the beck and call of all others, especially those most in need. Jesus is once again trying to get through to them that 'the Son of Man did not come to be served but to serve and give his life as a ransom for many'. Our God waits on us in every moment, and bends before us, even kneeling before us to wash our feet. Our God expects, even demands, that we do the same for all others. We are to give our life, moment to moment, day to day, as a ransom. To 'ransom' is to exchange something for another – in this case, our abundant life for the lack in the lives of others. This is the way of the Son of Man, the way of the cross, the way of power for those who are true friends of Jesus.

QUESTIONS

1. Most of us don't want to think of ourselves as the servant and are repelled by Jesus' insistence that we take this attitude on board. Often our repulsion is backed up by our view of those who are still treated as servants and slaves in our world – those who pick, process or package our food, clean our hotel rooms, serve meals in restaurants, manicure our lawns, even take care of our children. There are many who take on the jobs we do not want to do. Who in your family, your parish and neighbourhood needs a servant to help them, someone to exchange places with them for a day or help them with their lives? Can you do it more easily and more effectively with others?

2. Who are leaders in your parish, diocese, national Church that are good models for what Jesus is telling us we must be if we are to exert power in his community? Remember, they don't necessarily have to be ordained, credentialed, paid, professional, or belong to any religious community – good servants often aren't the ones most visible or even recognised in a community.

3. Why would you want to be a servant or a slave of Jesus? How can you go about learning how to do this in the world today from him? Who do you want to do it with?

Thirtieth Sunday in Ordinary Time

READINGS
JER 31:7-9; PS 126; HEB 5:1-6; MK 10:46-52

> Only those who walk in darkness ever see the stars.
> ALICE VERONICA MCKENNA, MY NANA

> O Christ, our Morning Star, Splendor of Light Eternal, shining with
> the glory of the rainbow, come and waken us from the greyness of
> our apathy and renew in us your gift of hope. Bring me into your
> presence that I may listen to your voice, which is the source of all
> wisdom, and watch your face forever. Amen.
> BEDE THE VENERABLE

These last Sundays before the Feast of Christ the King, the end in
Ordinary Time, and the end of the year seek to make us look at our lives
over the past year and see if we have indeed repented, been converted
and now follow Jesus more closely as a disciple with others in a
community. The Gospel introduces us to Bartimaeus, son of Timaeus,
once a blind beggar on the side of the road outside Jericho. He is
named and so most likely he is a member of the Markan community
and his story is known. His name has been noted to mean 'son of
fear' (timid) or 'son of the honoured one', though he certainly isn't
at this stage of his life. The story begins with him hearing that Jesus
of Nazareth is coming. In fact, practically all of our stories begin with
hearing of Jesus, or hearing his words. Bartimaeus is crying out over
the din of the crowd, trying to get Jesus' attention. He calls him Son
of David and cries for pity. But what happens next is most disturbing:
many of the crowd and the disciples of Jesus rebuke him (that word
again – one of harshness and rejection). Others are trying to decide
who gets to Jesus and who doesn't.

But Jesus hears, so he stops and has those who have rebuked
Bartimaeus call him over. Their tune changes drastically – now the
words are: 'Take courage, Jesus is calling you.' Jesus is seen to be the
champion of the discarded and cast-off, those not considered worthy

of coming near to God. Jesus is a healer and a friend to all those who are beggared, broken and lacking not only health, but acceptance in the community – and this is in spite of the lack of concern by his own followers, who are sightless and without any sense of Jesus' pity. In all the Gospels, being blind is to be hard-hearted, or unaware, or refusing to understand what Jesus is teaching. And the readings in the past weeks show Peter, James and John, the favoured circle of Jesus' followers, going blind in regard to what Jesus is attempting to make them see – his coming rejection, suffering and death in Jerusalem, the fate of all the prophets.

Bartimaeus does something remarkable! He gets up from the ground, throws off his cloak and runs to Jesus! His cloak is his protection, his house, if you will, that covers him from the harsh gaze of others. And he runs blind! He knows the voice! He stands before Jesus and Jesus' question to him is simple: 'What do you want me to do for you?' It seems obvious – he is blind and he wants to see again. The last word, 'again', reveals much. Bartimaeus wasn't always blind. Now he is given what he asks for – his faith has made him well, whole again. His seeing again is both physical sight and inward seeing, knowing and accepting Jesus. Earlier in the Gospel, Jesus has been cajoled by James and John as they blindly bid for positions of power, authority, prestige and honour. This man wants to see Jesus. And the closing line seals it – he begins to follow Jesus on his way. Jesus' way is the way of the Father, the way of the reign of God's justice, peace and forgiveness, the way of the cross. Bartimaeus, now a disciple, follows Jesus towards Jerusalem – unlike many of Jesus' inner circle who are with him but not following him on his way. He is now part of the community.

The reading from Jeremiah is about roads and about God gathering the remnant of the people to bring them home: the lost, the widows, the mothers, the pregnant, the blind and the lame. God leads them back to water and to where they will not stumble and fall. Their cries will be turned into psalms of praise in honour of their God, who is a father to them – each of them considered as though they were a firstborn child. Jeremiah's language paints an icon of the Jesus of Mark's Gospel, and the blind beggars and others we will meet in these readings tell us who is really a disciple. They teach Peter, James, John and us how to hear, to see and to come after Jesus.

This story is the bridge linking Jesus' teaching and his entry into Jerusalem with the conflict that intensifies between him and his final rejection and suffering. We are confronted with the question: who are we acting like? Are we like Jesus' inner core of disciples who are intent on their own way, ignoring and rejecting what they do not want to hear from Jesus? Or are we like Bartimaeus, asking that we might truly see Jesus, leap forward in faith and turn to follow him, all the way to the cross and glory? Our God is patient and understanding with us and yet we are pushed to make a commitment and honour it as well. The time grows short as this year turns once more.

QUESTIONS

1. In the baptismal liturgy there is much symbolism of light and darkness, of sight and blindness – in fact the sacrament was often called the Sacrament of Illumination. Being baptised meant changing as drastically as a person moving from blindness to sight. How is your eyesight of faith at the moment? Do you see Jesus going up to the cross and asking that we accompany him?

2. The crowd and Jesus' disciples who think they are close to Jesus can't see him as suffering, and so they are not very good at seeing others who are suffering. They are quick to keep those who both need Jesus desperately and are deeper in faith than themselves from getting to Jesus. Do you have companions that sometimes keep others from getting near Jesus? Or have you ever been blocked by others in your attempts to get to Jesus? What was it like and what can you do to make sure that it doesn't happen again?

Thirty-first Sunday in Ordinary Time

READINGS

DEUT 6:2-6; PS 18; HEB 7:23-28; MK 12:28B-34

> None of the philosophers before the coming of Christ could, by bending all effort to the task, know as much about God and things necessary for eternal life as after the coming of Christ, a little old woman knows through her faith.
>
> THOMAS AQUINAS

> As a magnifying glass concentrates the rays of the sun into a little burning knot of heat that can set fire to a dry leaf or a piece of paper, so the mysteries of Christ in the Gospel concentrate the rays of God's light and fire to a point that sets fire to the spirit of man.
>
> THOMAS MERTON

We are going back to basics, to our roots as believers, today. Specifically, we are going back to our Jewish roots in the law. In a sense there is only one law or commandment – the Shema: 'Hear O Israel! The Lord is our God, the Lord alone!' And it is followed by the commandment on how to respond to the reality of the existence of the Lord who is God alone: to love with all our heart, our soul and our strength. All the other statutes and commandments that Moses speaks about in the book of Deuteronomy follow from this one commandment and, in obeying it, one lives in fear of God and will know long life. It is a life of absolute loyalty to God alone, who is holy and deserving of all worship and obedience. It is supposed to be a love that springs from gratitude for all that God has done and continues to do for us. The people were encouraged to 'take these words to heart'– to engrave them on their minds, to memorise them, know them intimately and let them suffuse every muscle, bone, thought, action and relationship. They were to belong only to this God and no other.

This is the backdrop of the discussion between the scribes and Jesus. They are arguing over what the law means, interpreting and deciding what is expressed and expected. At the time of Jesus there were 613 prohibitions or demands and sometimes it was difficult to connect them to the one commandment of the Shema. When Jesus is questioned by the scribe, he quotes Moses – the core of Jewish law. We are to love God with everything we are and have: our life, our mind, our senses and our possessions (the meaning of strength) – and we are to do it faithfully all the days of our lives, with nothing held back. But Jesus adds in the second commandment: 'You shall love your neighbour as yourself' and he reiterates that there are no other commandments greater than these. He makes the two commandments into one: you are to love your neighbour with all your heart and soul and mind and strength.

The scribe compliments Jesus and adds on that God wants this kind of life as a sacrifice, not burnt offerings and other ritual proscriptions. Obedience and fulfilment of the commandment must be love in action not just words or prayers. Jesus compliments in return, but also surprises him with the observation: 'You are not far from the kingdom of God.' What? One wonders if the scribe became a follower of Jesus? Did he mull over the words and walk away? Did he balk and stick with what he had been studying all these years? The ending doesn't bode well: 'No one dared to ask him any more questions.' We are left with the question ourselves: are we still only 'not far from the kingdom of God?' Do our sacrifices of ritual, of liturgy, of prayer, fasting and devotions only get us to the edge of Jesus' kingdom? What do we have to do to step over the line and into Jesus' world? Is our obedience born of gratitude and found in every nook and corner of our lives? For us, to love our neighbour is to love our God and that is the completeness of practice – God cares more about our love of others than any love we profess to have for God! Today we are invited to step into the presence of God's love and obedience in Jesus. Have we made that leap of faith and practice?

QUESTIONS

1. Mark Twain once said: 'One of the nicest things that can happen to a person is to do good by stealth and to be found out by accident.' Do you believe that is true? Is this part of loving our neighbour and our God with all our heart and soul and strength? Talk about it and see what you learn from others.

2. The Jewish community still prays the Shema daily. Do you begin your day by looking in the mirror and reminding yourself that you are to live this day loving God and everyone with all your heart, soul, mind and possessions? Or what would it be like to look at yourself in the mirror and imagine Jesus saying to you: 'You are not far from the kingdom of God?' Are there others you'd like to take with you as you step into Jesus' immediate presence and power?

Thirty-second Sunday in Ordinary Time

READINGS

1 KGS 17:10-16; PS 146; HEB 9:24-28; MK 12:38-44 OR 41-44

> St Brigid's monastery in Kildare was known as the City of the Poor, because of its reputation for hospitality, compassion and generosity. God loves a true faith in him with a pure heart. Once Brigid had embarked on a journey and stopped by the wayside to rest. A wealthy woman heard that she was in the locality and brought her a basket of apples. As soon as the apples appeared, a group of people came by and begged for food. Brigid gave them the apples. Her giver was unhappy: 'I brought these apples for you, not for them.' Brigid replied: 'What's mine is theirs.'
>
> ANON.

> For what use is it when you give as much of wealth as someone might give a spoonful of water from the ocean, and you don't imitate the widow's generosity of spirit?
>
> JOHN CHRYSOSTOM

These last Gospels of the year tell us stories that are foundational, and in this story we are told to observe, with the other disciples, what true discipleship and following Jesus really looks like. And it's a very unlikely sight. In the long form of the Gospel, Jesus begins by warning the crowd about the scribes' way of being religious: taking the first places of honour, wearing robes that are distinctive to make them stand out, bowing and scraping in public and in the synagogues, and saying long prayers, all while taking the livelihood of widows. This public display of religiosity will reap 'a very severe condemnation' for the benefit of the eyes of others and what we might get from it.

We then hear what is called 'the widow's mite', when in reality it is the exact opposite. That title only fits if you consider the widow and her gift from the point of view of amount, if you are wealthy. From the point of view of Jesus it is the extravagant gift of the widow – the gift of her whole livelihood and life. Jesus observes those going into the temple and what they're putting in for the upkeep and refurbishment of its buildings and grounds. Lots of rich folks give large sums of money – one would know because it would make a distinctive sound as it dropped into the box. A widow puts her offering in too, some coins worth a few cents at most, then Jesus summons his disciples and asks them to observe her and her actions.

We usually use the word 'observe' not only to denote seeing, but also to signify obeying a law. Jesus wants his disciples to obey his commands and to live out his style of worship and care for others like the widow does. He gives her an enormous compliment by just noting what she has done: 'Amen, I say to you, this poor widow put in more than all the other contributors to the treasury. For they contributed from their surplus wealth, but she, from her poverty, has contributed all she had, her whole livelihood.' In short, Jesus says that she gives like he gives – her whole life and what she needs to sustain her life. It all is given over to God and God sees her and her gift as true worship.

There is another nameless widow in the Elijah story and she isn't even Jewish. She is an outsider, yet in obeying the laws of hospitality she is willing to share her last bit of flour and oil with the prophet, preparing it as a last meal for herself, her child and Elijah. Her gift is taken and God extends that gift so that there is enough food for a year and none of them go hungry. The two widows of our Scripture stories are bound in a number of ways. They are bound to God in their generosity and their hospitality, their openness to the other and to God. They are bound in poverty. They are bound in the depth of their obedience as they struggle to just survive day to day. And they are bound to the God of the poor, the God of life and the God that sees and knows all things and is close to them, delighting in how they mirror his own care, compassion and obedience to God in Jesus.

My nana once told me that the measure of a gift depends not so much on what is given or what it means to the one who receives it, but on what it has cost the giver. This is the way God looks at giving too, it seems. Elijah is given bread and oil, enough for a year, fed on the hospitality of the poor widow and her child and the graciousness of God. We too are fed on the bread of Jesus, the Eucharist for all our days, whether we give to God the bread and wine of our lives or not. When we gather for liturgy, we offer bread and wine – our bodies and lives – and we give a collection for the poor. In exchange we are given the Bread of Life and the Wine of the Spirit. As the bread and wine becomes the Body and Blood of the Lord, we become the Body of Christ and the Blood of hope and joy for others. And today we are left with the question: do we ever really give like the widow or like God gives, out of our very sustenance and source of life? Or do we give out of our surplus or not give anything much at all? Do we ever give Jesus great delight so that he'd like to use us as an example of what it means to truly come after him?

QUESTIONS

1. The widow of Zarephath fed a stranger and a prophet, willing to share the last of what she had. Who do we share our food with that may afford us a glimpse of God's power and presence for months to come?

2. Jesus warns the crowd about people who perform their religion for public consumption; for privilege; for place in society; for others' esteem and respect, while not doing justice, let alone caring for the poor. How can we remember that God cares not for our religious displays and devotion but cares passionately about how we treat widows, orphans, immigrants, strangers, migrants and those whose lives are precarious and close to the edge in society?

3. What would it mean for you to 'once in a while' give like the widow did? Who or what cause would you give it to? Would you be delighted to give it secretly so that it was between you and God?

Thirty-third Sunday in Ordinary Time

READINGS

DAN 12:1-3; PS 16; HEB 10:11-14, 18; MK 13:24-32

> I know that this life, missing its ripeness in love, is not altogether lost.
> I know that the flowers that fade in the dawn, the streams that strayed in the desert, are not altogether lost.
> I know that whatever lags behind, in this life laden with slowness, is not altogether lost.
> I know that my dreams that are still unfilled, and my melodies still unstruck,
> > are clinging to Your lute strings, and they are not altogether lost.
> > > RABINDRANATH TAGORE

> Prayer is meaningless unless it is subversive, unless it seeks to overthrow and to ruin the pyramids of callousness, hatred, opportunism, falsehoods.
> > RABBI ABRAHAM JOSHUA HESCHEL

This is the last Sunday in Ordinary Time and the readings are apocalyptic in nature. This is often thought to mean predictions about the end times that instil fear and trembling, but that's not really what they are intended for. Rather, they are intended to be encouragement to those under persecution at present. The Gospel begins with the phrase 'in those days' being used by the prophets and with Jesus announcing terrible signs in the heavens with the sun, moon and stars in disarray. It is true that in both the reading from Daniel and in the Gospel, the times are described as 'unsurpassed in distress', but every generation could give you such a litany of disasters. But this Gospel is also a declaration of the coming of the Son of Man in glory, to gather all the elect from the ends of the earth and to judge the nations with justice. What we often neglect in grappling with these readings is the hope, the coming glory and the power that is stronger than any of these events. This experience is rooted in the reality of the present. Jesus is on the Mount of Olives as he declares what is to come, and this is the same place that he will be praying on the night he will be tortured before being condemned to death by crucifixion. And it takes place immediately before he enters the city for the last time.

We are told to remember and learn a lesson from the fig tree: when its branch becomes tender and sprouts leaves, you know that summer is near. In the same way, when you see these things happening, know that he is near, at the gates. He is near, at the gates! We are to stand up and take heart! This is how we are to prepare for the end of time, for the end of a year, for the end of an era, for the end of a government, nation, political regime or economic system – the end of everything, for everything eventually ends or dies. And we are told that 'no one knows the day or the hour not the angels or even the Son, only the Father'. The focus is not on the when, but on how we are to live in expectation and hope, witnessing to the alternative that Jesus' presence and words have wrought in the world, in the will of God for justice and peace for all and abundant life for all here upon earth now.

The fig tree is the strongest symbol in both of the Testaments for the reign of God, the promise come true among peoples, the reality of peace among all nations. We are to watch for the signs of justice and peace and know that the fullness of God's favour and grace is near. God's dreams for all people will be close to coming true; there will be salvation and judgement. And in the meantime, 'heaven and earth will pass away' but this generation (then and now) will not pass away and Jesus' words will not pass away – this is reality now, whether it is recognised as such or not. Every generation must live through 'their world' passing away – their institutions, states, ways of living, cherished realities of 'the way things are', even in religion and Church. There will be endings without number before whatever the mystery and the culmination of life on earth and in our universe will be. What is crucial is to live now with truthfulness and integrity, as the Body of Christ, and pray and live for the coming of the will of God and God's kingdom here in all circumstances and in all realities.

The question is: if the words of Jesus were to come to pass now, would we be found written in the book? Would we be found among those who shall be an everlasting horror and disgrace, or are we the wise that shall shine brightly like the splendour of the firmament? Today and any day, no matter what is happening in history, is a time of blessing and hope for those of us who stand with Jesus before the temples and powers of the world but serve the justice and peace of God. We do this knowing that we will, with Jesus, fall on our knees begging for strength to endure what comes, because we seek to be faithful to Jesus' Word of Truth. But we believe that we will rise in glory with the Crucified and Risen Lord of Life. Today, and as the liturgical year comes to an end, we will commit ourselves to God as the power that contradicts all history and we will stand together to build a future of grace and freedom out of our present day – no matter what challenges our time might present to us.

QUESTIONS

1. Jesus' prayer, words, works and presence is subversive no matter what is going on in the world because Jesus stands for the Father's way of liberation and love. Do we resist the dominating structures of society and work for the Father's children worldwide, in all times and circumstances? We stand with Jesus, but who else do we stand with?

2. The description in Daniel is magnificent, it sings! How do we as individuals, as small communities and as Church need to live in the world today so that we are such stars and beacons of hope and life in the midst of distress, wars, destruction and ecological disasters?

3. Who are your stars? Are we signs of hope, like the fig tree, getting ready to burst forth into bloom and bless all those around us in every season? In this past year, have we become words of hope and the light of Good News for others in need of courage?

Christ, King of the Universe

READINGS

DAN 7:13-14; PS 93; REV 1:5-8; JN 18:33-37

> [Christ the King] has shared his power so that by serving him in
> others, [his followers] might through humility and patience lead their
> brothers and sisters to that King whom to serve is to reign. For the
> Lord wishes to spread his kingdom of means of the laity, a kingdom
> of justice, love and peace ... the faithful, therefore, must learn the
> deepest meaning and value of all creation, and how to relate it to the
> praise of God. They must assist one another to live holier lives even
> in their daily occupations. In this way the world is permeated by the
> spirit of Christ and more effectively achieves is purpose in justice,
> love and peace. The laity have the principle role in the universal
> fulfilment of this purpose.
>
> VATICAN II

> One can never wrestle enough with God if one does so out of pure
> regard for the truth. Christ likes us to prefer truth to him because,
> before being Christ, he is truth. If one turns aside from Christ to go
> towards the truth, one will not go far before falling into his arms.
>
> SIMONE WEIL

The year of the Lord, 2012, comes to an end this week. We gather our
days and nights, our lives with all their lacks and dreams to stand before
our God, the Son of Man, a criminal of the Roman Empire, a prophet
rejected by his own, Jesus our Crucified King, who is the Truth. One
day, all nations, peoples and languages will know the truth and stand
before him in glory and his dominion will be everlasting. But while
on earth, Jesus stood before the dominating powers as a criminal, and
he would be in the same place today. Jesus stands in solidarity with
the poorest, the least, those who never make it in the structures of
society. He stands with those who destabilise the dominance of the
world's institutions by their presence and their need. Today we are
confronted with a simple and devastating question: who do we belong

to, who lays claim on us? Do we stand with Jesus, with the Truth of God, and with those Jesus stands with, or do we stand on the other side that decides who lives and who dies, uses violence and fear to manipulate reality, decrees what is acceptable in society? Perhaps we waffle back and forth, sometimes in collusion with the powers that be, and sometimes inching closer to Jesus' side? When we look back over this year of the Lord, 2012, where were we to be found and how did others know where we stood?

Jesus' kingdom does not belong to this world in the sense that it operates or comes into being as kingdoms do in history. Jesus' reign is that of justice, of peace, of abundant life, of forgiveness, of mercy and love as God has loved us, of truth. Jesus is clear: 'For this I was born and for this I came into the world, to testify to the truth. Everyone who belongs to the truth listens to my voice.' This is the reason why we were born and why we are in this world too – to testify to the truth – and we do this by listening to and obeying the Word of Jesus, following that Voice, standing with him and living in solidarity and communion with those he stands close to, lives with and dies with. We are guarded by, protected by, live under the loving gaze and tender regard of the Truth of God.

One day there will be the fullness of peace, abiding justice and freedom and liberation – life in God for all. For now, we stand in those corners, pockets and places in the world where God's reign has been planted and is blooming like weeds, in spite of what might be happening all around. We make our stand, we hope for a dearer life and we link arms and hands with all those who listen to the Word steadfastly, believing that this new way of living, this revolution of love and peace exists now, here among us, and that our God stands with us in the power of the Spirit in the presence of our Crucified and Risen Lord. It is the only place we will stand and the only God we will worship, bend before and serve – in all our brothers and sisters – with our God looking back at us in the face of every human being, even now. We are Jesus' kingdom, his presence and hope for the world, even now. We are God's delight and glory, even now. We hang on for a dearer life, for God's will for life to come in fullness, but we taste it, even now.

We belong to 'the Alpha and the Omega, the one who is and who was and who is to come, the almighty'. God is always coming towards us!

QUESTIONS

1. Another year is coming to a close for us as believers in Jesus. Take some time to look over this past year of your life. Would you be ready to present this year and your life to God as service rendered, as witness to your solidarity with the least of our brothers and sisters, and as a gift to God in gratitude for all that has been given to you? Or would you like another year?

2. We stand before Jesus, the Truth, and Jesus looks at us and wants to know if we stand with him? Can he rely on us to stay with him through the hard times and to be with him in solidarity with those who suffer innocently? Who would you want standing with you today?

3. To call Jesus a king can be problematic in our world, since it is usually not a positive symbol of the use of power or authority or protection. What would you rename this feast on the last Sunday of each year? What title/s do you think Jesus would use for this feast? Think back to the many we have heard in his Voice over this past year.

Select Bibliography

Arnold, Eberhard, ed., *The Early Christians: In Their Own Words*, Rifton, New York: Plough Publishing House, 1998.

Benson, Robert, *Between the Dreaming and the Coming True: The Road Home to God*, New York: Tarcher, 2011.

Bernier, Paul, *Bread Broken and Shared: Broadening our Vision of Eucharist*, Notre Dame: Ave Maria Press, 1981.

Bonhoeffer, Dietrich, *The Cost of Discipleship*, New York: Touchstone, 1995.

Buber, Martin, *The Way of Man: According to the Teaching of Hasidism*, New York: Citadel, 2000.

Cather, Willa, *Death Comes for the Archbishop* (1927), London: Virago, 1995.

Hellwig, Monika K., *Jesus: The Compassion of God*, Collegeville, Minnesota: Liturgical Press, 1988.

John Paul II, for the XXVI Annual World Day of Prayer for Peace, 'If You Want Peace, Reach Out to the Poor', 1 January 1993.

Merton, Thomas, *Life and Holiness*, New York: Image, 1969.

Merton, Thomas, *Seeds of Contemplation*, Norfolk, Connecticut: New Directions Books, 1949.

Merton, Thomas, *When the Trees Say Nothing*, Kathleen Deignan, ed., Notre Dame: Sorin Books, 2005.

Stringfellow, William, *A Keeper of the Word: Selected Writings of William Stringfellow*, Bill Wylie Kellermann, ed., Grand Rapids, Michigan: Wm. B. Eerdmans Publishing Company, 1994.

Tagore, Rabindranath, 'Not Altogether Lost', *The Heart of God: Prayers of Rabindranath Tagore, Selected and Edited by Herbert F. Vetter*, North Clarendon, Vermont: Tuttle Publishing, 1997.

US Bishops' Pastoral Letter on War and Peace, 'The Challenge of Peace: God's Promise and Our Response', 1983.

Various, *Watch for the Light: Readings for Advent and Christmas*, Rifton, New York: Plough Publishing House, 2001.

Walsch, Neale Donald, *Tomorrow's God: Our Greatest Spiritual Challenge*, London: Atria Books/Simon & Schuster, 2003.

Weil, Simone, *Waiting For God*, New York: Harper Perennial, 1992.